# THE MAILBOX® CLASSROOM MANAGEMENT

**grades 1-3**

**SUPER SIMPLE!**

## Quick Tips and Timesaving Reproducibles for the Whole Year

P9-CAY-794

- Classroom setup
- Routines and procedures
- Positive discipline
- English language learners
- Organizing paperwork
- Parent conferences
- Welcoming new students
- Time fillers
- Center management
- and MORE!

Over **175** management tools to choose from!

**Managing Editor:** Kelly Robertson

**Editorial Team:** Julia Alarie, Becky S. Andrews, Randi Austin, Diane Badden, Pamela Ballingall, Amber Barbee, Michelle Bayless, Brooke Beverly, Jennifer Bragg, Kimberley Bruck, Karen A. Brudnak, Tracy Combs, Pam Crane, Chris Curry, Colleen Dabney, Kathryn Davenport, Mary Davis, Beth Deki, Lynn Drolet, Karen Favor, Amanda Graham, Heather Graley, Tazmen Hansen, Terry Healy, Marsha Heim, Lori Z. Henry, Deborah Horn, Laura Johnson, Krystle Short Jones, Debra Liverman, Kitty Lowrance, Coramarie Marinan, Beverly McCormick, Laura Mihalenko, Farrah Milby, Brenda Miner, Suzanne Moore, Lisa Mountcasel, LaVone Novotny, Jennifer Nunn, Jennifer Otter, Mark Rainey, Hope Rodgers, Deborah Ryan, Eliseo De Jesus Santos II, Rebecca Saunders, Kelly Smith, Rosemary Smith, Hope Spencer, Donna K. Teal, Rachael Traylor, Sharon M. Tresino, Teresa Vilfer-Snyder, Christine Vohs, Jamie Vought, Sue Walker, Carole Watkins, Brenda Wilke, Zane Williard, Virginia Zeletzki

## www.themailbox.com

©2010 The Mailbox® Books
All rights reserved.
ISBN10 #1-56234-926-0 • ISBN13 #978-1-56234-926-4

Printed in the United States
10 9 8 7 6 5 4 3 2 1

HPS 211909

# What's Inside

**PRACTICAL tips** for successful classroom management

Check out an "Editor's Pick" when you need an idea in a hurry!

## Parent Conferences

✓ **Editor's Pick**

### Sail Through Conferences
Use the acronym shown to remind you of key points to discuss during a parent conference. Write notes on a copy of page 80 to assist you during the conference. Then complete the remaining sections of the form during or after the conference.

**S** = Share three positive observations.
**A** = Acknowledge areas of student's strengths.
**I** = Inform the family of concerns.
**L** = Listen to the family's comments, questions, and concerns.
**S** = Set goals for the student.

### Wristband Reminders
Make a class supply of the watch patterns on page 81, cut them apart, and label each one with a different student's name. Then write the date and time of each child's parent conference on a watch. The day before a scheduled conference, tape each student's watch around his wrist to wear home.

### A Worthwhile Welcome
To create an atmosphere that will make conferences a positive experience for parents, try these tips.
- Display your name on the door for parents to easily locate your room.
- Set up a waiting area with chairs, textbooks, or other materials of interest for parents who arrive early.
- Display a sample of each student's best work.
- Group chairs to form a meeting area where you and the parents can sit together comfortably and share their child's work.

### "Tea-rific" Parents
Guide each child to fold a 6" x 12" piece of paper in half horizontally and make three cuts in the top half to create four equal flaps. On each flap, have the student draw a picture that shows why her parent is terrific and, under each flap, write a sentence about the picture. Lead each student to wrap the paper around a foam drinking cup, tape the ends together, and put a tea bag inside the cup. Give each cup to that child's parent on conference day.

See page 81 for a conference request form and page 82 for a thank-you letter to send home after a conference.

*Super Simple Classroom Management • ©The Mailbox® Books • TEC61256* 79

**TIMESAVING** assessments, checklists, patterns, and more

### How Am I Doing?

Name _____ Date _____

Use the code to give yourself a grade for each of the following areas.

**Code**
1—I'm doing great!
2—I'm doing well.
3—I'm having some trouble.
4—I'm not doing well at all.

| Subject | Grade | Subject | Grade |
|---------|-------|---------|-------|
|         |       |         |       |
|         |       |         |       |
|         |       |         |       |
|         |       |         |       |

I am most proud of _____

I need to work on _____

My behavior is _____

Note to the teacher: Use with "Progress Review" on page 39. Fill in subject areas on a copy of this page before making student copies. 41

**Thank-You Cards**

## Thank You
"Berry" Much!

I appreciate all your hard work.

Sincerely,

*Super Simple Classroom Management • ©The Mailbox® Books • TEC61256*

## THANKS
for being a "Grrrreat" Volunteer!

I appreciate all your hard work.

Sincerely,

*Super Simple Classroom Management • ©The Mailbox® Books • TEC61256*

**Bookmark Patterns**
Use with "Homework Bookmarks" on page 67.

Hop Into a Good Book!

Read, Read, Read!

68

*Super Simple Classroom Management • ©The Mailbox® Books • TEC61256*

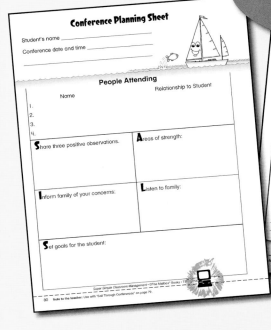

Reproducible forms and notes you can CUSTOMIZE online

Look for this symbol!

Full-color tools that you simply PULL OUT AND USE

# Table of Contents

# Before the First Day

# Bulletin Boards and Displays

## Up for the Year

For each child in your class, fold a sheet of construction paper in half and cut out a rectangle to make a frame. Unfold the paper and program it with an encouraging phrase, such as "Great job!" "So neat," or "I love it!" When a student completes an assignment you're both proud of, place it behind a frame and staple it to a board. Periodically update students' samples.

## Equal Opportunities

Program a copy of the checklist from page 7 with students' names. Keep the list near a designated good-work display. As you post a child's work, write the date in the corresponding row and column. Refer to the checklist when you post work to ensure that each child has had an assignment on the display.

## A Welcoming Display

Enlarge the crayon box pattern on page 8 and program it with your name and grade level. Next, copy the crayon pattern on page 8 to make a class supply. Cut out the crayons and write each child's name on one. Then attach the crayon box to your classroom door and arrange the crayons around the box. Later in the school year, take the crayons off the door and hang each one on a bulletin board with the corresponding student's work.

## Brilliant Borders

Add some sparkle to a bulletin board by stringing seasonal lights around its perimeter. Or hang seasonal garland, tinsel, or beaded fringe around the border for other eye-catching options.

# Displayed Work Checklist

| Student Name | Reading | Language Arts | Math | Other |
|---|---|---|---|---|
|  |  |  |  |  |
|  |  |  |  |  |
|  |  |  |  |  |
|  |  |  |  |  |
|  |  |  |  |  |
|  |  |  |  |  |
|  |  |  |  |  |
|  |  |  |  |  |
|  |  |  |  |  |
|  |  |  |  |  |
|  |  |  |  |  |
|  |  |  |  |  |
|  |  |  |  |  |
|  |  |  |  |  |
|  |  |  |  |  |
|  |  |  |  |  |
|  |  |  |  |  |
|  |  |  |  |  |
|  |  |  |  |  |
|  |  |  |  |  |

**Note to the teacher:** Use with "Equal Opportunities" on page 6.

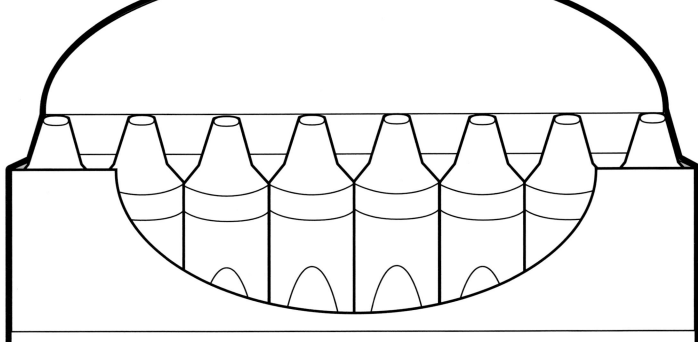

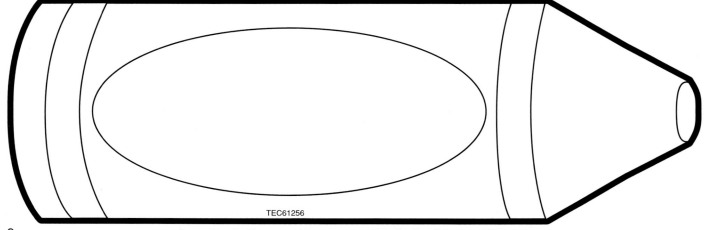

Welcome to the Pack!

TEC61256

TEC61256

**Editor's Pick**

## Easy Maintenance

After you have organized a center, your library, or any other area that students use, take a photo of it. Then place an enlarged copy of the photo in a plastic sheet protector near the designated area. After students use the area, they can refer to the photo to return materials to their proper places.

## Check the Dots

Use sticky dots to let students know which items are available to use during free time. Attach green sticky dots to things students can use at any time, yellow sticky dots to items students must ask permission to use, and red sticky dots to items students are not permitted to use. Students simply check the dots to make their free-time choices!

## Ready for More

As you personalize items such as nametags or folders for students, set aside a few blank ones in case new students join your class later in the year. Place the items and your welcome letter in a large mailing envelope. Add other materials as the year progresses. If a new student joins your class, the materials you'll need will be ready in one place!

## A Future Reference

When you need a break from setting up your room, visit your colleagues' classrooms. Take photos of how they've set up their desks, centers, or carpet areas. Be sure to include the teacher in at least one photo so you'll have a reference for each room. Share the photos with the teachers you visited and keep a set for yourself to refer to when you're ready for a change.

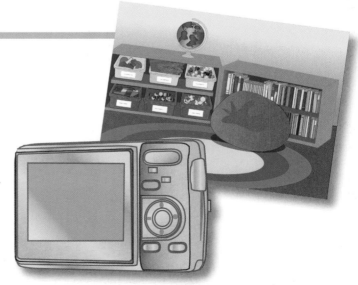

**Editor's Pick**

### Grab-and-Go Center

Short on space for centers? Stock a shower caddy or a tool bag with materials and handouts for a center. Instruct a child to take the container to the workspace of his choice.

## More Room for Books

To free space inside students' desks, provide one plastic shoebox-size container for each group of students. Label a card with each group's name and then use clear Con-tact paper to secure it to one end of the box. Have students place inside the box crayons, scissors, rulers, and other basic materials needed to complete classroom activities. Direct each group to keep its box in the middle of its workspace. Or, to avoid distractions, stack the boxes in a designated space until needed.

Just "Ripe" Contractions

## Hang It Up

Label each of several large resealable plastic bags with the name of a bulletin board or center. Place corresponding materials in each bag; then clip the bag to an inexpensive pant hanger. Store the hangers in a closet in the order in which you'll use them. If desired, also place in each bag a photo of the completed display or center and a list of the materials needed.

## Signed Out for Safety

To know at a glance who's out of the room, label a sheet of paper as shown and laminate it. Post the sign near your classroom door. Then use a Velcro fastener to attach a dry-erase marker to the sign. When a child leaves the room, direct him to write his name in the appropriate column and then wipe it clean when he returns. Should a safety drill occur, you'll have all your students accounted for.

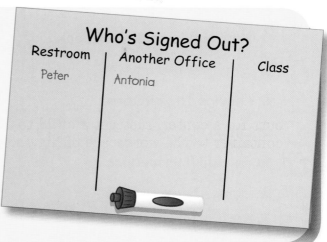

## Attendance Indicator

Label a large sheet of construction paper as shown; then laminate it for durability. Post the sign in an accessible location. Write each child's name on a clothespin and place it around the bottom section. Upon his arrival, direct each child to move his clip to the top section. After reporting attendance, remove any clips from the bottom section and use them to hold students' absence work.

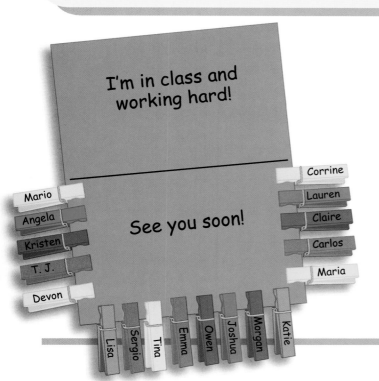

## Motivate for Mastery

Enlarge a copy of the procedures checklist on page 12 and check the procedures you would like to establish in your classroom. Then post the checklist where all students can see it. Explain that you would like students to master the checked procedures by a given date. Each week, review the list with students and highlight the procedures the class has mastered. Give a small prize to the class when a predetermined number of procedures are highlighted and a more desirable reward if students meet your goal by the deadline.

See page 13 for ready-to-use hall and restroom passes. Simply use a permanent marker to write your name on each one; then cut them out!

# Establish Your Classroom Procedures

Check the procedures you want to teach your new class.

- ☐ ☆ Entering the classroom
- ☐ ☆ Hanging up coats and bookbags
- ☐ ☆ Starting the day
- ☐ ☆ Leaving the classroom
- ☐ ☆ Lining up
- ☐ ☆ Fire drill procedure
- ☐ ☆ Using the restroom
- ☐ ☆ Dismissal
- ☐ ☆ Getting a drink of water
- ☐ ☆ Heading papers
- ☐ ☆ Asking a question
- ☐ ☆ Walking in the hallway
- ☐ ☆ Lunchtime procedures
- ☐ ☆ Sharpening pencils
- ☐ Getting supplies
- ☐ Turning in homework

- ☐ Working at a center
- ☐ What to do with unfinished work
- ☐ Asking for help
- ☐ Outdoor recess
- ☐ Indoor recess
- ☐ Throwing away trash
- ☐ Playing with the class pet
- ☐ How to use free time
- ☐ Working in a group
- ☐ Completing makeup work
- ☐ Using the classroom library
- ☐ Using a classroom computer
- ☐ Other: _____
- ☐ Other: _____
- ☐ Other: _____
- ☐ Other: _____

**Tips for you**

✔ For each procedure you checked, list two to four steps you want students to follow.

✔ Teach students the starred procedures first.

✔ Practice each procedure with students.

✔ Display reminders of the main procedures.

*Super Simple Classroom Management* • ©The Mailbox® Books • TEC61256

12    **Note to the teacher:** Use with "Motivate for Mastery" on page 11.

# Hall Pass

_____'s Class

# Hall Pass

_____'s Class

# Restroom Pass

_____'s Class

# Restroom Pass

_____'s Class

# Hall Pass

_____'s Class

TEC61256

# Hall Pass

_____'s Class

TEC61256

# Restroom Pass

_____'s Class

TEC61256

# Restroom Pass

_____'s Class

TEC61256

# At the Beginning of the Year

## Classroom Rules

1. Treat others the way you want to be treated.

2. Keep hands, feet, and objects to yourself.

3. Walk quietly in the hallway.

4. Respect yourself and your classmates.

5. Always do your best work.

Kyle

Kelly          Marcus      Lupe

Gabriel      Susy

Javier

## Homeward Bound

To foster a smooth transition at the end of the first day and to build math concepts, post a grid similar to the one shown. Have each child place a personalized sticky note on the grid to show how he intends to get home. The resulting graph is a ready-to-go math lesson and an at-a-glance chart for dismissal!

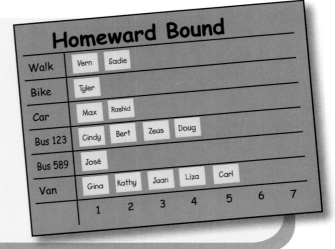

| Homeward Bound | | | | | | | |
|---|---|---|---|---|---|---|---|
| Walk | Vern | Sadie | | | | | |
| Bike | Tyler | | | | | | |
| Car | Max | Rashid | | | | | |
| Bus 123 | Cindy | Bert | Zeus | Doug | | | |
| Bus 589 | José | | | | | | |
| Van | Gina | Kathy | Juan | Liza | Carl | | |
| | 1 | 2 | 3 | 4 | 5 | 6 | 7 |

## Safety First

Guide youngsters to conclude that they can learn anything in a safe classroom. Then help them write a description of a physically and emotionally safe classroom environment. Have each child sign the document to show he agrees to be safe in the classroom. (For ideas that help establish classroom rules, see pages 21–23.)

## Getting Acquainted

Label a Venn diagram with headings such as those shown. Then invite each child to attach a personalized copy of a pencil card from page 18 in the appropriate location on the diagram. Discuss the finished diagram as a way for students to get acquainted. If time allows, repeat the activity with topics such as owning sneakers or sandals, liking spelling or math, and preferring magazines or books. Adapt the activity for a T-chart using topics such as having or not having pets, liking or disliking pizza, and riding or not riding the bus.

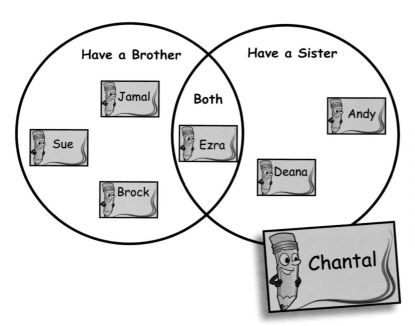

## Partner Pages

Have pairs of students complete this book project as a way to get to know each other. (For an odd number of children, partner yourself with a student.) Instruct each child to write, draw, and label a page that describes her partner. Compile the completed pages in a class book and then place it in your reading area for a selection that is sure to be reread often!

Jeremiah has brown hair. He has three cats.

Nicole is nice. She likes dogs.

## Human Sort

For a skill-based icebreaker, secretly select a characteristic by which to sort your students, such as eye color, number of letters in one's name, or shoe type. Then direct students into groups without telling them how they are being sorted. Encourage youngsters to share their observations in order to determine the rule of the sort.

Reach for the Stars!

Our Class Goal — When in the hallway, we will walk in line quietly.

## Reach for the Stars!

To develop student responsibility, write a class goal on a copy of page 19 and post it in a child-friendly location. At the end of the day, ask youngsters to help you decide whether the goal was met. If so, invite a child to color a star. When each of the stars is colored, celebrate the class's success as desired.

## Read and Share

Tell your students about a favorite storybook. After sharing why the story is one of your favorites, invite youngsters to settle in for a read-aloud of the book. Then help children learn more about each other by having them make personal connections to the story.

See page 20 for a checklist to help you prepare for the first day of school.

# Pencil Cards

Use with "Getting Acquainted" on page 16.

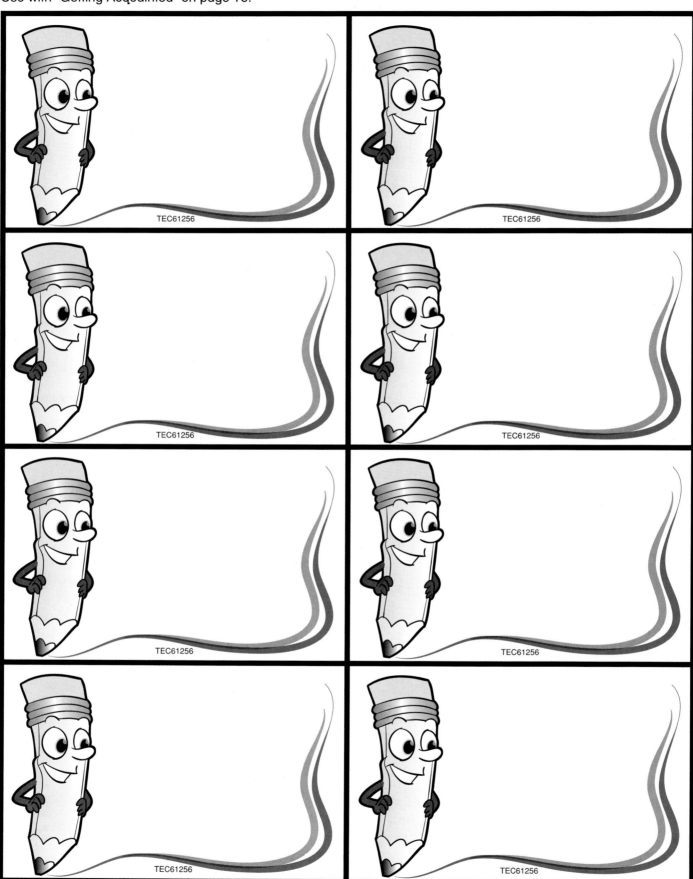

# Reach for the Stars!

Our Class Goal

*Super Simple Classroom Management* • ©The Mailbox® Books • TEC61256

# Getting Ready for the First Day

Highlight each step that applies to your classroom setup; check the star or box once you complete the task.

☆ Post emergency evacuation route(s)

☆ Obtain student information
- ☐ Class list
- ☐ Emergency contact numbers
- ☐ Health-related concerns (asthma, allergies, etc.)
- ☐ Special needs

☆ Put up displays
- ☐ Welcome sign
- ☐ Bulletin boards
- ☐ Wall displays

☆ Set up centers

☆ Set up class library

☆ Sharpen pencil supply

☆ Gather supplies
- ☐ Chart paper
- ☐ Dry-erase markers or chalk
- ☐ Audio equipment
- ☐ Computer equipment
- ☐ Digital camera
- ☐ Other: _____
- ☐ Other: _____

☆ Write lesson plans

☆ Post weekly schedule

☆ Set up for attendance

☆ Set up for lunch order

☆ Put nametags on student desks or workspaces

☆ Put nametags on student cubbies or coat hooks

☆ Post calendar

☆ Prepare job chart

☆ Prepare weather chart

☆ Submit classroom repair work orders

☆ Write substitute teacher plans

☆ Other: _____

☆ Other: _____

☆ Other: _____

☆ Other: _____

☆ Other: _____

☆ Other: _____

☆ Other: _____

*Super Simple Classroom Management* • ©The Mailbox® Books • TEC61256

# Establishing Classroom Rules

## Monster Rules!

To inspire interest in establishing and following classroom rules, tell a story about an unruly monster that once visited the classroom. The monster broke most—maybe all!—of the guidelines you use to manage your classroom. Lead students to conclude that such behavior is unwelcome. Then guide youngsters to create a list of rules to follow. Have each child sign the resulting document to show his agreement with the rules.

### Classroom Rules

1. Treat others the way you want to be treated.
2. Keep hands, feet, and objects to yourself.
3. Walk quietly in the hallway.
4. Respect yourself and your classmates.
5. Always do your best work.

Kyle    Marcus    Lupe
Kelly         Susy
    Gabriel        Javier

## Rule-Following Photos

Demonstrate appropriate classroom behavior with digital pictures! Assign a different classroom rule to each student pair or small group. Have each pair stage and then take a snapshot of the desired behavior. Instruct each pair to write a caption for its picture. Post the resulting visual aids with the title "Model Behavior."

Be polite to others.

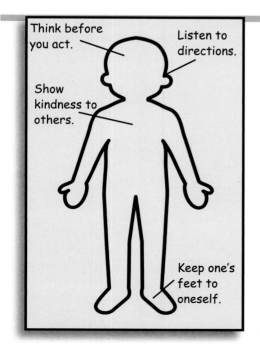

Think before you act.

Listen to directions.

Show kindness to others.

Keep one's feet to oneself.

## Body-Part Rules

Students are the perfect props to generate classroom rules! To begin, draw a simple body outline on a sheet of chart paper. Then name a body part and lead students to determine a rule for it. For example, a rule for the brain might be "Think before you act" while one for the heart could be "Show kindness to others." Have students point to the corresponding body part and write the rule by that location on the outline.

### On the Map

Lead a discussion about classroom rules. Then display the rules on a thinking map like the one shown. If desired, assign a different rule to each of several small groups and have them illustrate the behavior. Post each illustration by its corresponding rule.

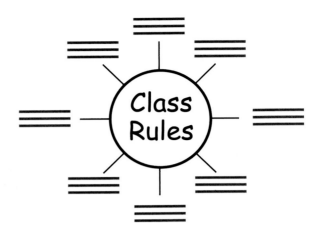

Class Rules

### R-E-S-P-E-C-T

Have each youngster write one way he might demonstrate respect to others or how he would like to be shown respect. Display the completed papers. Then have students work together to list four or five statements that summarize students' ideas on how to maintain a respectful classroom environment.

We the children

### We the Children

Have youngsters create a classroom constitution that features class rules and expectations. First, discuss student and teacher expectations. Use the information to form a classroom constitution and have each child sign the document. Then tear the edges and color them brown to make it look like an ancient scroll.

### Attention!

To quickly get students' attention, establish this classroom rule. Announce a predetermined phrase or sound for which students should listen. Each time they hear you call out the phrase, students repeat it, look at you, and wait for the announcement.

Ribbit, ribbit!

See page 23 for a reproducible contract to help you establish student support for classroom rules.

# Count Me In!

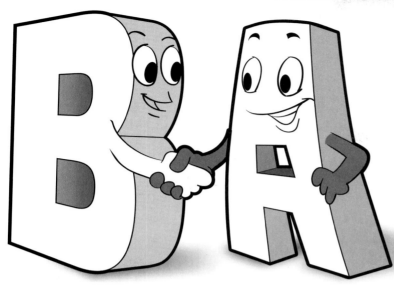

 Our safe classroom is important to me.

 I want to learn.

I will follow our classroom rules.

_____

student signature

_____

teacher signature

*Super Simple Classroom Management* • ©The Mailbox® Books • TEC61256

---

# Count Me In!

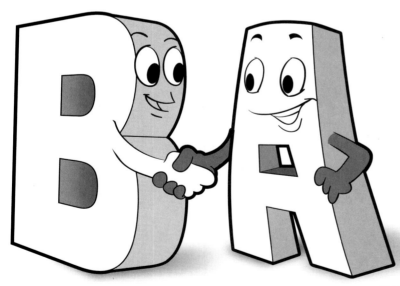

 Our safe classroom is important to me.

 I want to learn.

I will follow our classroom rules.

_____

student signature

_____

teacher signature

*Super Simple Classroom Management* • ©The Mailbox® Books • TEC61256

---

**Note to the teacher:** Make a copy of the student contract for each child. After reviewing the classroom rules together, have each child sign a contract to show his willingness to abide by the rules, and then add your signature.

# Open House

### Editor's Pick

I have black hair and green eyes. I have big feet. I like to eat pizza.

Robert

### Game Time!

Try this icebreaker to welcome parents! Prior to open house, have each child write his name on a sheet of paper. On the reverse side, instruct him to draw a self-portrait or write a personal description. Put the papers on students' desks name side down or display them on a bulletin board. When parents visit the room, encourage them to find their child's paper, checking the name to confirm the match.

## Family Matters

Gather interesting family news while sending a clear message that you are genuinely interested in getting to know each child. Place a copy of the student information sheet on page 26 on each student's desk. During open house, ask each family to respond to the questions. For families who are unable to attend, send the sheet home for a family member to complete and return the next day. If your open house is held before school starts, consider mailing the sheets in advance for families to submit when they visit the classroom.

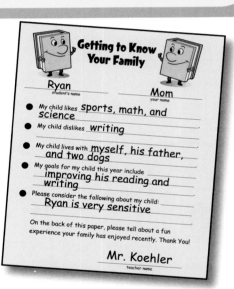

### Getting to Know Your Family

Ryan
student's name

Mom
your name

- My child likes **sports, math, and science**
- My child dislikes **writing**
- My child lives with **myself, his father, and two dogs**
- My goals for my child this year include **improving his reading and writing**
- Please consider the following about my child: **Ryan is very sensitive**

On the back of this paper, please tell about a fun experience your family has enjoyed recently. Thank You!

Mr. Koehler
teacher name

---

Dear Dad,
Do you like my desk? It's really clean! I knew you would be surprised!

Love,
Wyatt

## Please Write Back!

Get students excited about open house with this letter-writing activity. Have each child write a letter to a family member who he thinks will attend and have him leave the letter on his desk. During open house, ask a family member (preferably the one addressed in the letter) to respond. Be sure to write a reply yourself for students whose families are unable to attend. Start the next school day by giving students time to read their letters!

## Where and When?

To cut down on repetitive questions during open house, provide visual aids that give the answers. Display simple posters, labels, and schedules to show information such as lunchtime, library day, center locations, volunteer requests, music class, and dismissal procedures.

## Purposeful Puzzle Pieces

Surprise each youngster with a personal message the day after open house! Draw puzzle pieces on a large sheet of bulletin board paper (one piece per student plus one additional piece). Write "Welcome!" on a center piece. During open house, invite families to write a message to their child on a puzzle piece. Be sure to write a message to each student whose family is unable to attend. Then puzzle-cut the banner and place each child's personalized piece on his desk. The next day, after students read their messages, have the class work together to assemble the unique class puzzle.

## Wish Fish

Need extra supplies for activities? Try this! Write on fish cutouts the materials you need and store the cutouts in a fishbowl. Explain how you will use the materials to support instruction. Then invite each family to take a fish and return it to school with the requested item. Be sure to replenish the bowl as needed throughout the year.

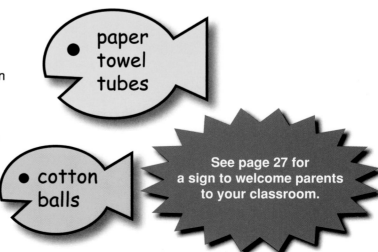

See page 27 for a sign to welcome parents to your classroom.

# Getting to Know Your Family

_____   _____
student's name                              your name

● My child likes _____
_____.

● My child dislikes _____
_____.

● My child lives with _____
_____.

● My goals for my child this year include _____
_____
_____.

● Please consider the following about my child: _____
_____
_____.

On the back of this paper, please tell about a fun experience your family has enjoyed recently. Thank You!

_____
teacher name

_Super Simple Classroom Management_ • ©The Mailbox® Books • TEC61256

26   **Note to the teacher:** Use with "Family Matters" on page 24.

# Welcome

_____'s

to

# Grade!

_____

Super Simple Classroom Management • ©The Mailbox® Books • TEC61256

# All Year Long

### Work Saver

At the beginning of the school year, create a hanging file folder for each student and place the folders alphabetically in a storage crate. If a child is absent, place any makeup work in his folder. When the student returns, he checks his folder and completes any work he missed.

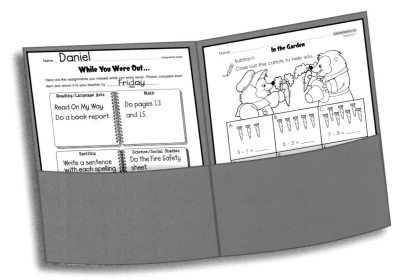

### While You Were Out

Label the front of several two-pocket folders with "We Missed You." Inside each folder, place a copy of the form on page 31. When a student is absent, place one of the folders on his desk. During the day, place any missed work in the folder. Before sending the folder home, write information about the assignments on the enclosed form. If the child is absent more than one day, add a new form for each day and continue to gather the missed work in the folder.

### It's in the Mail

Create individual student mailboxes from shoe storage boxes or use another paper-filing system. When distributing graded papers or handouts, slip each one into its owner's box. At the end of the day, gather the paperwork from each absent child's box, stack it on top of her homework, and add any directions needed to complete the work. Then staple the papers along with a colorful copy of one of the cards on page 32.

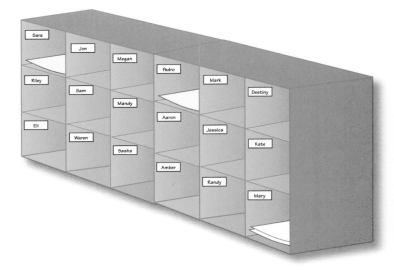

# While You Were Out...

Here are the assignments you missed while you were away. Please complete each

item and return it to your teacher by _____.

date

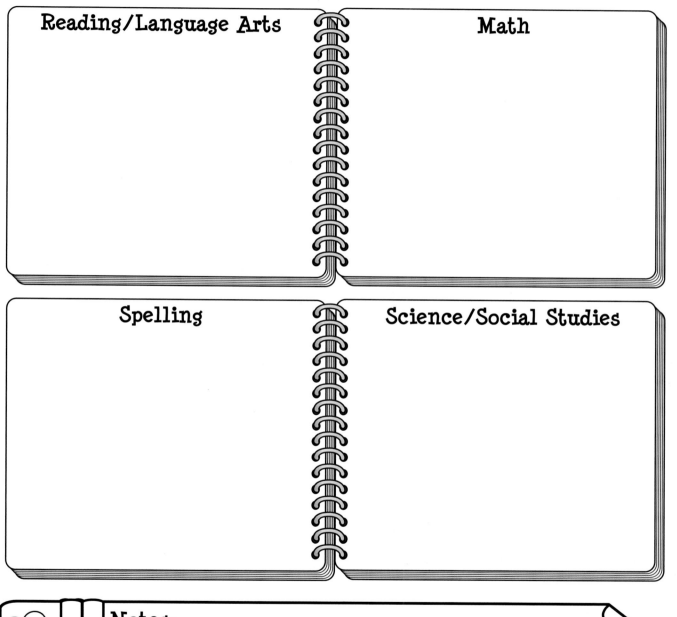

Reading/Language Arts

Math

Spelling

Science/Social Studies

Notes:

Super Simple Classroom Management • ©The Mailbox® Books • TEC61256

**Note to the teacher:** Use with "While You Were Out" on page 30.

31

## Our class won't be "purr-fect" until you return!

TEC61256

## Our school just isn't the same without you!

### Get well soon!

TEC61256

## Glad you're back—

### we can't bear to be without you.

TEC61256

## Sorry you're not feeling well.

### Hope you'll hop back to school soon!

TEC61256

**Editor's Pick**

## Clip It

To keep assignments and directions organized for classroom volunteers, tape a clear plastic page protector to the back of a clipboard. In the pocket, place a completed copy of the form on page 34. On the front, clip the assignments the volunteer needs to work on with an individual student. If the adult has a question about what to do, she turns the clipboard over to read your notes.

## Buddy Up

If you have students who need extra reading practice, invite school staff members into your classroom to become reading buddies. Enlist cafeteria workers, custodians, and office personnel to volunteer for 15 minutes once or twice a week. Pair each adult with a child and have him provide encouragement as he listens to the student read.

## What to Do?

To cut down on interruptions by volunteers, place two baskets on a small table or desk near the door. Label one basket "To Do" and the other "All Done." In the first basket, place tasks and projects that need to be completed along with the directions and supplies needed to complete the jobs. Instruct each volunteer to choose a task from the first basket to work on and place the finished project in the second basket.

To Do          All Done

See page 35 for thank-you notes to give to classroom volunteers.

# Volunteer To-Do List

_____
date

**1.**

**2.**

**3.**

**4.**

**5.**

**6.**

**7.**

**8.**

**9.**

**10.**

# Thank You
## "Berry" Much!

I appreciate all
your hard work.

Sincerely,

_____

# THANKS
## for being a
## "Grrrreat" Volunteer!

I appreciate all
your hard work.

Sincerely,

_____

# Arrival and Dismissal

## Graph It

Turn arrival time into a graphing opportunity. Glue each child's photo to a personalized card and stick a magnet to the back. Post a different question and a graph on a magnetic board near the door each morning. Write possible answers to the question on the graph. As each student arrives, she places her card beside her response to the question. Use the resulting graph to take attendance as well as jump-start a class discussion.

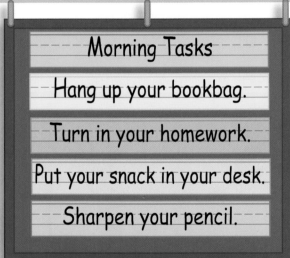

| What is your favorite pet? | | | | | |
|---|---|---|---|---|---|
| **cat** | Marco | Sofia | Ana | Olive | |
| **dog** | Jacob | Max | Lupita | Spencer | Thomas |
| **fish** | Alex | | | | |
| **hamster** | Emily | Tristan | | | |
| | 1 | 2 | 3 | 4 | 5 |

### Morning Tasks

Hang up your bookbag.

Turn in your homework.

Put your snack in your desk.

Sharpen your pencil.

## Ready for the Day

Give students an at-a-glance reminder of their morning responsibilities. Program sentence strips with different tasks you'd like students to perform, such as those shown. Each morning, slip the appropriate strips into a pocket chart.

## Hit a Home Run

To help students get ready for the end of the school day, teach them the acronym *HITS*. Use the key shown to remind them to straighten up and collect hand-outs, classwork, clothing items, and homework assignments to take home.

| | |
|---|---|
| **H**ome = | Do you have everything you need to take home? |
| **I**tems = | Do you have all your personal items? |
| **T**omorrow = | Are you prepared for tomorrow? |
| **S**pace = | Is your space neat and clean? |

See page 37 for a form to keep track of how students go home.

# How We Get Home

Teacher: _____

Grade: _____

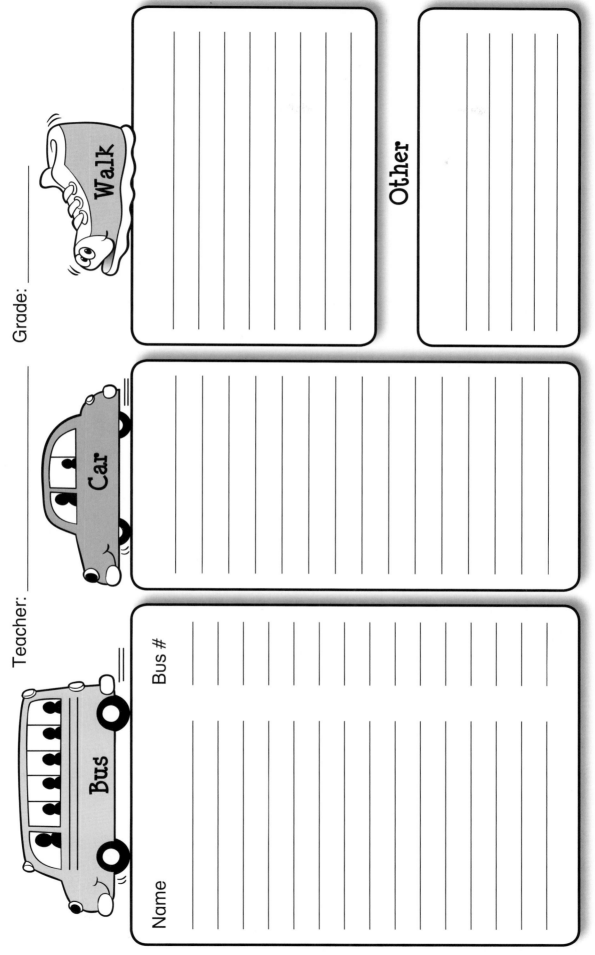

**Bus**

Name _____ Bus # _____

**Car**

**Walk**

**Other**

*Super Simple Classroom Management* • ©The Mailbox® Books • TEC61256

**Note to the teacher:** Write each child's name in the appropriate column. Add the students' bus numbers if they are bus riders. Post the list in the classroom as a reminder of how each child gets home.

## Progress Review

Before the end of each grading period, meet with each student individually to discuss how he views his progress. Next, have him complete a copy of page 41. After you review the student's self-evaluation, place one copy in his assessment folder and send another copy home with his report card to inform his parents about how he views his school performance.

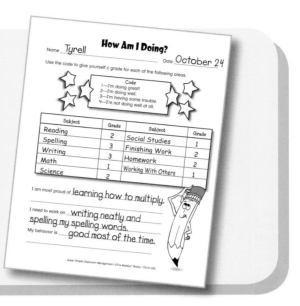

## Revisiting Skills

After grading a test, compile a list of the three to five most common mistakes. Before the next test in that subject, review the listed errors with the class. Then include one or more similar tasks on the upcoming test.

## Stick With It

Prepare a clipboard for taking anecdotal notes by sticking small sticky notes in rows on several sheets of paper clipped to the board. Throughout the day, jot observations on separate notes labeled with the observed student's name. At the end of the day, move each note to the corresponding student's file.

## Show-and-Tell

Have your students place samples of their classwork throughout the week in personalized folders. At the end of the week, invite each child to review her folder and select her best piece of work. Meet with small groups so each child can show her selection to classmates and share why she chose it.

See page 39 for a sign to post during testing and page 42 for a list of report card comments.

# Shhhh...

## Testing is in progress.

# How Am I Doing?

Name _____ Date _____

Use the code to give yourself a grade for each of the following areas.

### Code
1—I'm doing great!
2—I'm doing well.
3—I'm having some trouble.
4—I'm not doing well at all.

| Subject | Grade | Subject | Grade |
|---------|-------|---------|-------|
|         |       |         |       |
|         |       |         |       |
|         |       |         |       |
|         |       |         |       |
|         |       |         |       |

I am most proud of _____

_____

I need to work on _____

_____

My behavior is _____

_____

# Report Card Comments

## Academic

- is making progress in all academic areas
- is a hard worker and takes pride in his or her work
- has improved in _____
- is having difficulty with _____; the following suggestions might help him or her improve _____ _____

## Work Habits

- is an attentive listener
- responds well to directions
- is a hard worker
- is showing improvements in _____
- is showing interest in and enthusiasm for the things we do
- works well in a group setting
- has strong organizational skills
- needs to actively participate in class discussions
- is having difficulty with organizational skills

## Behavior and Responsibilitiy

- has a great attitude
- is always kind and helpful to other students
- is cooperative and is pleasant to be around
- is learning to occupy his or her time constructively
- has had difficulty listening during class and is often distracted when working on assignments
- has difficulty working and cooperating with his or her classmates
- has difficulty completing assignments
- has difficulty turning in assignments on time

# Birthdays and Celebrations

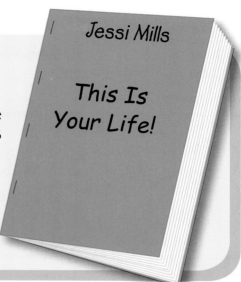

Jessi Mills

This Is Your Life!

## This Is Your Life!

The week before a student's birthday, prepare a blank booklet titled "This Is Your Life!" Label a booklet page for each year of the child's life. Then send the booklet home, instructing family members to add pictures and descriptions about the child's life on each year's page. The child returns the book to school and shares it with the class on her birthday. Assign each student with a summer birthday a day during the school year on which to share her book.

## Draw a Gift!

Help each child feel extra special on his birthday by presenting him with a simple, no-cost gift! In advance, program the blank cards on a copy of page 44 with additional appropriate gifts, such as lunch with the teacher, lunch with a friend, or extra center time. Make a desired number of copies, cut apart the cards, and place them in a gift bag. On a student's birthday, have him draw one slip out of the bag and then present him with the matching gift!

## Be the Best Guest!

Give students a handy reminder of party behavior by teaching them this simple verse. Then, when you want students to display these skills, prompt them by holding up your hand and saying, "Be the best guest!"

| | |
|---|---|
| I am saying "please" and "thank you." | *Hold up pointer finger.* |
| I am taking turns. | *Hold up pointer finger and middle finger.* |
| I am sharing. | *Hold up pointer finger, middle finger, and ring finger.* |
| I am talking quietly. | *Hold up four fingers.* |
| I am the **best guest** I can be! | *Hold up four fingers and thumb.* |
| Give me five! | *Raise your hand high.* |

See page 45 for birthday cards to present to students and a party supply request form.

## "Whoooo" has a birthday today?

You do!
Happy birthday!

TEC61256

## Hats off to you on your birthday!

Hope it's a happy one!

TEC61256

Dear Parent,

This year, our class will be having several parties. If you would be willing to donate a refreshment or supply for one of our parties, please indicate your preference below. Then complete the form and return it to school as soon as possible. I will contact you several days before your donation is needed. Thank you in advance for helping make our parties more successful!

Sincerely,

_____

I would be willing to donate

☐ _____  ☐ _____
☐ _____  ☐ _____
☐ _____  ☐ _____

My child's name: _____
My name: _____
Phone number: _____

*Super Simple Classroom Management* • ©The Mailbox® Books • TEC61256

45

Editor's Pick

## Spotting Great Assignments

Have each student personalize and cut out a construction paper copy of a giraffe pattern from page 47. Each time a student completes an assignment neatly and on time, invite him to color a spot on his giraffe. When a child has colored all the spots on his giraffe, reward him with a small prize.

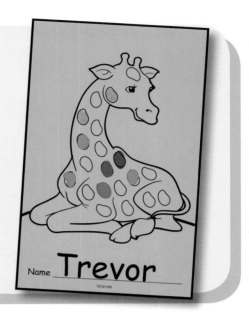

Name Trevor

## Keep It Neat!

Encourage students to keep their desks tidy and their supplies organized with this incentive. From time to time when students are out of the room, check their desks for neatness and organization. Slip a small treat into each desk that meets your expectations.

## Responsibility Buddies

Invite students to help each other become more responsible. Pair students (and participate yourself if you have an odd number of children). Have the partners prompt each other to record homework assignments, remind each other when important projects are due, and make sure they have the proper books and materials packed at the end of the day. Reminding their buddies also helps students recall the important information themselves.

Don't forget our science projects are due tomorrow!

Name _____

TEC61256

Name _____

TEC61256

### Editor's Pick

### Keeping Track

To keep students' center work on track, program a copy of the checklist on page 53 with center names, due dates, and free choice activities for early finishers. Give each child a copy; then instruct him to put a check mark in the "Completed" column alongside each center he finishes.

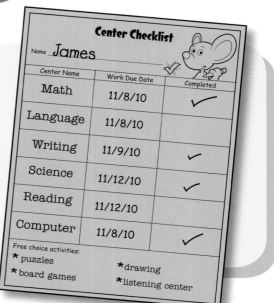

**Center Checklist**

Name James

| Center Name | Work Due Date | Completed |
|---|---|---|
| Math | 11/8/10 | ✓ |
| Language | 11/8/10 | |
| Writing | 11/9/10 | ✓ |
| Science | 11/12/10 | ✓ |
| Reading | 11/12/10 | |
| Computer | 11/8/10 | ✓ |

Free choice activities:
* puzzles
* board games
*drawing
*listening center

### Center Rotation

To simplify center management, laminate a large card stock card for each center area. Use a wipe-off marker to program each card with several student names. Then post each list in a center. Throughout the week, move each list to a different center. At the end of the week, reprogram each list for the next week's center rotation cycle.

### Color-Coded Centers

Here's a way to have centers even if there's no room to spare in your classroom. Choose a different-colored folder for each center. Place in each folder a class supply of the center activity printed on colored paper to match the folder. Then place the folders in an accessible location along with the necessary supplies to complete each assignment.

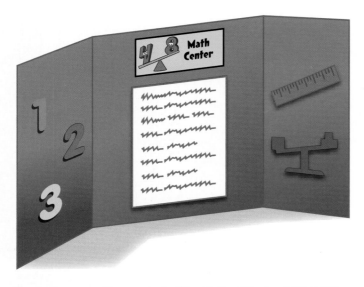

### Instant Centers

Decorate a cardboard display board with a center label (see pages 49 and 51) and related die-cuts or pictures. Post a center activity on the display board. Then position the board near a worktable with the necessary materials nearby.

Math Center

TEC61256

Writing Center

TEC61256

Reading Center

TEC61256

# Language and Spelling Center

TEC61256

# Computer Center

TEC61256

# Science Center

TEC61256

# Center Checklist

Name _____

| Center Name | Work Due Date | Completed |
|---|---|---|
| | | |
| | | |
| | | |
| | | |
| | | |
| | | |

Free choice activities:

*          *

*          *

**Note to the teacher:** Use with "Keeping Track" on page 48.

53

### Editor's Pick

### Collection Time

Decorate and label a box lid to use as a homework collection tray. Each week assign the job of collection agent to one student. Then have your collection agent wear a special cap as he gathers his classmates' homework and places it in the tray.

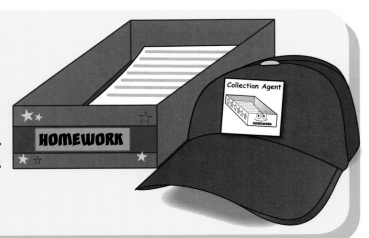

### Daily Delivery

Build more teaching time into your day by enlisting the help of a student as your classroom mail carrier. Establish a classroom mail center with a section for each child. Place in a mock mailbag homebound student papers (folded and labeled for privacy). Before dismissal, have your mail carrier file each paper in the corresponding section of the mail center.

### Check Out or Check In

Add the task of library assistant to your job list. Station your assistant in the library area with a class list containing a row of boxes next to each name. When a child borrows a book, the library assistant marks an *O* in the box next to the child's name. When the book is returned, he marks an *I* in the next box.

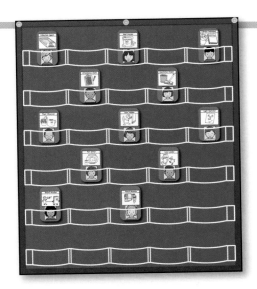

### Classroom Helpers Chart

Glue a copy of each job card from pages 56 and 57 onto the upper portion of a tagboard card as shown. (For a description of each job, see page 55.) Place the cards in a pocket chart; then put a different child's photo below each job card to designate your helpers. When it's time for new jobs, simply rearrange the photos.

# Helping Hands

## CHECK OUT THIS HANDY LIST OF UNIQUE AND TRADITIONAL JOBS!

 **Collection agent:** collects class homework

 **Mail carrier:** distributes student work and parent notes in the classroom mail center for youngsters to take home

 **Library assistant:** straightens bookshelves and keeps track of classroom library books checked out and in by students

 **Sanitation helper:** sweeps and picks up trash

 **Attendance clerk:** takes class attendance

 **Board washer:** washes whiteboards or chalkboards

 **Plant observer:** checks classroom plants and waters them if needed

 **Line leader:** leads the class to its destination, modeling appropriate behavior

 **Door holder:** holds the door open as the group exits and enters the room

 **Pencil monitor:** sharpens pencils and empties the pencil sharpener

 **Light switcher:** turns lights off when the class leaves the room and on when the class returns

 **Pet sitter:** feeds the class pet

## Collection Agent

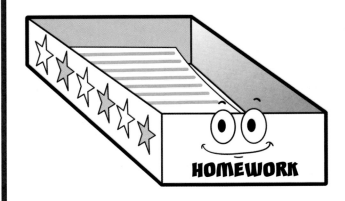

TEC61256

## Mail Carrier

TEC61256

## Library Assistant

TEC61256

## Sanitation Helper

TEC61256

## Attendance Clerk

TEC61256

## Board Washer

TEC61256

## Plant Observer

TEC61256

## Line Leader

TEC61256

## Door Holder

TEC61256

## Pencil Monitor

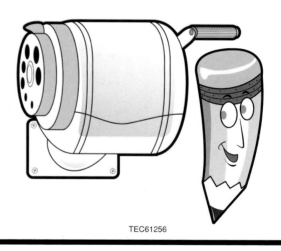

TEC61256

## Light Switcher

OFF

TEC61256

## Pet Sitter

TEC61256

### Editor's Pick ✓

## Shapely Organization

Organize your classroom library using die-cut shapes. Group books together by topic. Then label each of your book tubs with a corresponding shape, such as a pumpkin for Halloween-related books. Students use the symbols as a reference when searching for and returning books.

## Check It Out

Simplify your book checkout procedure with this easy-to-manage system. On each of several library pockets write a range of letters—such as "A–D," "E–H," etc.—to encompass the whole alphabet. Attach the pockets to the wall in an accessible location. When a student borrows a book, he writes his name and the book title on an index card and slips it in the pocket that corresponds with the first letter of the borrowed book's title.

## Brand-New Books

To add to your classroom library each year, try this! Before an event when parents will be visiting your classroom, such as open house, create a display similar to the one shown. On each apple list the title and author of a book you would like to have in your classroom library. Encourage any interested parents to take an apple from the tree and then donate the corresponding book to your class.

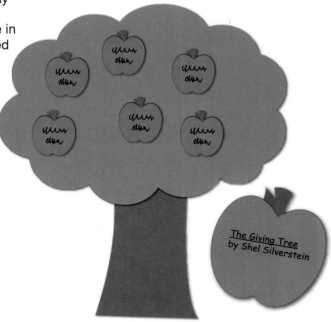

*The Giving Tree* by Shel Silverstein

See page 59 for a book form students can use as a follow-up to a class read-aloud or an individually read book.

# I Recommend This Book!

_____

book title

_____

author

**The characters are…**

**The setting is…**

**The plot is about…**

**This is a picture of my favorite character.**

**My favorite part of the book is…**

### Classroom Community

Have each student use construction paper to make a house or building and decorate it as desired. Display the completed homes and buildings on a bulletin board. Guide the class to brainstorm ways to create a caring community in the classroom; then list several ideas to implement as a classroom code of conduct. Have each student sign the code; then post it on the bulletin board.

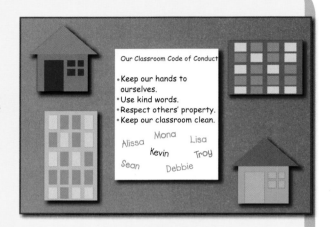

Our Classroom Code of Conduct

• Keep our hands to ourselves.
• Use kind words.
• Respect others' property.
• Keep our classroom clean.

Alissa  Mona  Lisa
Kevin  Troy
Sean  Debbie

## Getting to Know You

Initiate a feeling of classroom community at the start of a new school year by arranging all the desks (including yours) in a large circle to encourage interaction and bonding. Later, group the desks in smaller configurations to provide the same experience in smaller groups.

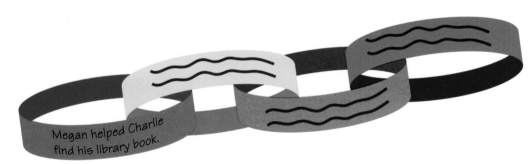

Megan helped Charlie find his library book.

## Catching Kindness

Write on a paper loop a child's name along with an act of kindness you caught her doing. Share the loop with the class and praise the child's actions. Explain that you are creating a community kindness chain and are secretly watching for acts of kindness. Then hang the first link on a wall to inspire behavior that builds a caring community. As children earn new links, add each one to the chain.

**Editor's Pick**

### Technology Tents

Have each child label and decorate the outside of a large, folded index card as shown to make a technology tent. On the inside of the card, have the student list usernames and passwords for programs that she accesses on the computer. When she uses the classroom computer, have the student place her technology tent nearby so her information is easily accessible. If you're taking the class to the technology lab, just grab the tents and distribute them when you arrive.

*Technology Tent*
*Keisha*

### Get Connected

Place a laminated copy of the computer sign-up sheet on page 62 in your computer center along with a wipe-off marker. When a student wants to use a computer, he writes his name on the list to schedule a turn. To reuse the sheet, simply wipe it clean with a baby wipe.

Class List

Amanda
Avery
Becton
Candace
David
Ferguson
Jacqueline

### Check Your Name

To keep track of which students have completed a required activity on the computer, clip a copy of your class list to a clipboard. Place the clipboard near your computer area. When a student finishes his work on the computer, he checks his name off the list. You'll know at a glance which students still need to complete the task!

# Get Connected!

Name: _____

Name: _____

Name: _____

Name: _____

Name: _____

Name: _____

**Note to the teacher:** Use with "Get Connected" on page 61.

### ✓ Editor's Pick

### Ring of Pictures

Invite an ELL student to attach a different sticker—such as an apple, a dog, and a frog—to each of several small blank cards. Help him identify each image; then label each card and hole-punch the top left corner. Secure the cards on a metal ring. Once the child can name each word, invite him to add new cards to his ring.

apple

### Say and Match

Place facedown on a table a set of picture cards showing school supplies, such as a pair of scissors, paper, a pencil, and a bottle of glue. Display the actual items nearby. Turn over a card and name the item. Encourage an ELL student to repeat the word; then have her match the picture to the corresponding item.

### Photo Opportunities

Fill a photo album with labeled pictures of classroom materials, daily events, and different areas of your school. Refer to the book throughout the day to help your ELL students learn new vocabulary and understand upcoming events.

Scissors

### What Is It?

Place a variety of items from a specific category, such as clothing or toys, in an opaque bag. Instruct an English-speaking classmate to hold the bag open; then invite an ELL student to remove an item from the bag. The classmate names the object and then encourages the ELL student to repeat the word. This activity helps build vocabulary *and* friendships!

**Editor's Pick**

## Field Trip Scavenger Hunt

Before going on a field trip, list on a copy of page 65 things you would like students to look for while they're on the trip. When you arrive at your destination, give each child a pencil and a copy of the list on a clipboard. As each child finds an item, she checks the corresponding box. When you return to school, invite youngsters to tell about the things they saw.

Name Holly

### Find It on the Field Trip

Student checklist

Check the box beside each item you find.

☑ Find the crocodile.
☑ Find the gorilla.
☐ Find a bear that likes to swim.
☐ Find a bird with pink feathers.
☐ Find a mammal with stripes.
☐ Find the longest snake you can.
☐ Find an animal that hops.
☐ Find the smallest animal you can.

Super Simple Classroom Management • ©The Mailbox® Books • TEC61256

Emma
Max
Kailey
Owen
Lexie
Seth

## Organized Lunches

When a field trip requires bag lunches, try this handy idea. Tape a different-colored paper circle to each of several plastic tubs. As each child places his lunch in a tub, stick a matching colored sticky dot on his nametag. When it's time to eat, call students by color to retrieve their lunches.

## In the Envelope

After passing out field trip permission forms, attach a class list to a large envelope. Place a list of emergency contact numbers and a resealable plastic bag of first aid supplies inside the envelope. As each child returns her permission form to school, highlight her name on the list and place her form inside the envelope. You'll know at a glance which students have not returned their permission forms. When it's time to leave for the trip, simply grab the envelope and you'll have everything you need!

Amy
Bruce
Cole
Heather
Ian
Micah
Nell
Olivia B.
Olivia T.
Penelope
Quincy
Rayna
Rayshawn
Sarah
Say'Quan
Todd
Tyler
Vivienne

See page 66 for a reproducible field trip evaluation form.

# Find It on the Field Trip

Check the box beside each item you find.

 _____

 _____

 _____

 _____

 _____

_____

_____

 _____

*Super Simple Classroom Management* • ©The Mailbox® Books • TEC61256

# What Did You Think?

Complete each sentence.

I really enjoyed _____

_____

_____

I did not like _____

_____

_____

Draw to show your favorite part of the trip.

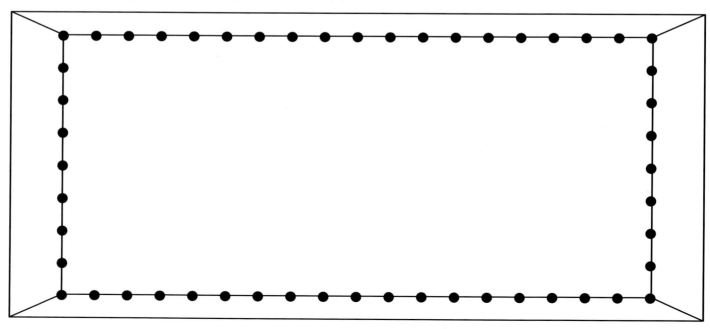

### Filing Assignments

Label a separate stacking tray for each subject plus one for miscellaneous work. In each tray place a laminated class list and a wipe-off marker. As each student arrives, he files his homework in the appropriate trays and then initials beside his name on the corresponding class lists. Not only will you be able to quickly tell who has turned in assignments, but homework papers will also be neatly sorted.

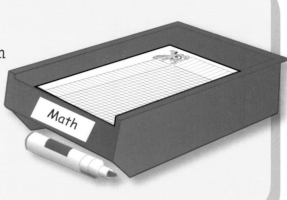

Math

Read, Read, Read!

### Homework Bookmarks

Give each student a copy of a bookmark from page 68. When a child completes a homework assignment on time, place a sticker or your initials on the bookmark's grid. When a child's grid is full, she gives you her bookmark to be laminated. Return the laminated bookmark to her along with a new bookmark and a small prize or homework pass.

### On a Hunt

Put a twist on traditional homework assignments by sending students on a scavenger hunt. Type a simple list of tasks related to skills you want to reinforce. Have each youngster complete the list at home with his family's help. This engaging idea encourages students to complete homework assignments and promotes family involvement.

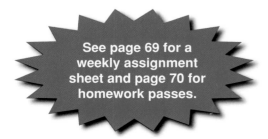

See page 69 for a weekly assignment sheet and page 70 for homework passes.

Name _____

**Homework Scavenger Hunt**

1. List six things at home whose names begin with a blend.

2. List the names of six things in your refrigerator in ABC order.

3. Divide the number 20 by the number of rooms in your home.

4. Tell about an item in your home that is a geometric shape.

5. Multiply the number of people in your family by 8.

Hop Into a Good Book!

Read, Read, Read!

TEC61256

TEC61256

# Weekly Homework Assignments

| Monday | Date: | |
| :--- | :--- | :--- |
| Special information: | | |
| **Tuesday** Date: | | |
| Special information: | | |
| **Wednesday** Date: | | |
| Special information: | | |
| **Thursday** Date: | | |
| Special information: | | |
| **Friday** Date: | | |
| Special information: | | |

## Upcoming Tests or Quizzes

## Reminders

## All-Star

Homework Pass

TEC61256

## Yippee!

No Homework Tonight

TEC61256

You deserve a break!

Enjoy this homework pass!

TEC61256

## Let's Celebrate!

This pass entitles

_____

to a homework-free evening!

**Homework Pass**

TEC61256

### Check the Can

To prepare, decorate a clean, empty Pringles potato chip can as shown. Copy pages 72 and 73 on yellow paper, cut out the potato chips, and place them in the can. When a student finishes his work before his classmates, he chooses a chip from the can and completes the task. Several times throughout the year replace the potato chips with new cutouts to vary the tasks.

Finished?

Check the Can!

List as many things as you can that come in pairs.

Make a graph that shows the number of boys and girls in the class.

### Stop and Go

Use red and green plastic cups to keep unnecessary interruptions to a minimum when you are working with a small group. Display the green cup when independent workers are free to ask you questions. Display the red cup when students must wait for your attention. Remind youngsters that no matter what color cup you are displaying, they may always interrupt you in case of an emergency.

### Personal Work Folders

Personalize a two-pocket folder for each child. Label one pocket "To Do" and the other pocket "Done." In the "To Do" pocket place incomplete or makeup assignments, review work, flash cards, or short reading books. During independent work time, the child selects items from the "To Do" pocket of her folder and moves them to the "Done" pocket as she finishes them.

# Potato Chip Patterns ● ● ● ● ● ● ● ● ● ● ● ● ● ● ● ● ● ● ●

Use with "Check the Can" on page 71.

Make a graph that shows the number of boys and girls in the class.

TEC61256

Choose ten things in the classroom and list them in ABC order.

TEC61256

Write a story about a time you were surprised.

TEC61256

Write the numbers backward from 100 to one.

TEC61256

Draw a Venn diagram. Use it to compare and contrast two animals.

TEC61256

Write a letter to a friend that explains why he or she should read a book you recently read.

TEC61256

Write a descriptive paragraph about your favorite food.

TEC61256

Write and solve three word problems.

TEC61256

*Super Simple Classroom Management* • ©The Mailbox® Books • TEC61256

List as many things as you can that come in pairs.

TEC61256

Find 12 items in the classroom that are a geometric shape. Draw each item and label which shape it is.

TEC61256

Write to describe your favorite room in your home.

TEC61256

Use the numbers 2, 4, and 6 to make as many math problems as you can.

TEC61256

Make a map of the school. Label each room.

TEC61256

Write a letter to the principal to convince him or her to give an extra week of summer vacation.

TEC61256

Write to explain the difference between wants and needs.

TEC61256

Find ten numbers in the classroom. Write the numbers from smallest to largest.

TEC61256

# Organizing Student Papers

### Stop and Go Folders

Label the pockets of a green two-pocket folder and the front of a red two-pocket folder for each child as shown. The red folder holds unfinished work and stays in the student's desk. At the end of the day, the student files graded papers in the appropriate pockets of her green folder and takes it home. Parents look for the green folder nightly. To help students remember which folder stays and which one goes, teach them the saying "Green can go home, but red must stay."

### Help Needed

When a child's completed work indicates that he needs additional help with a skill, file his paper in a "Follow-up Needed" folder. Each time you have a few free minutes, select a paper from the folder and meet with the corresponding student.

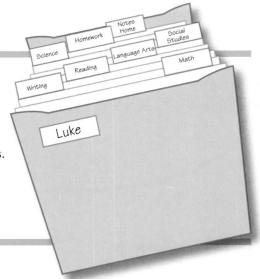

### A Handy File

Keeping up with a separate folder for each subject may not work for the organization-challenged child. Instead, ask his parents to purchase a letter-size accordion file that has seven to ten sections. Label each section with a different subject. The child can store his papers in one place with only one file to keep up with.

### Grab and Grade

Place a large filing box in a central location in the classroom. Label a file for each subject area. Alphabetically arrange the folders in the box. When a student completes his assignment, he places it in the appropriate folder. When it's time to grade papers, simply remove the desired folder from the box.

**Editor's Pick** ✓

## Everything You Need

For each skill you teach, file reproducibles and other paperwork in their own folder. Attach a copy of page 76 to the front of each folder, listing materials used to teach the skill and where the materials are stored. Also jot down ideas you have about adding to or changing your teaching of the skill. When you begin planning to teach the skill, you'll be able to locate the necessary materials quickly and implement new teaching ideas easily.

## Colorful Files

To make quick work of filing, attach a colored sticky dot to each drawer of your filing cabinet. Attach a corresponding-color sticky dot to each folder housed in that drawer. At a glance you can tell which drawer the folder belongs in.

## Reproducible Binders

Label a three-ring binder for each subject area you teach. Place dividers in each binder labeled with the corresponding skills. Then file a copy of each of your favorite reproducibles behind the appropriate divider. If a student needs extra practice with a particular skill, flip to a corresponding reproducible and copy it for her to complete.

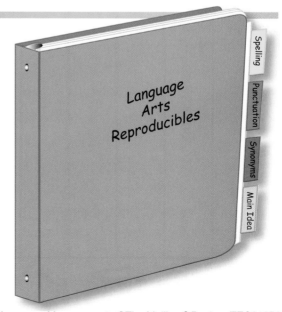

See page 77 for a class list and page 78 for a student information form.

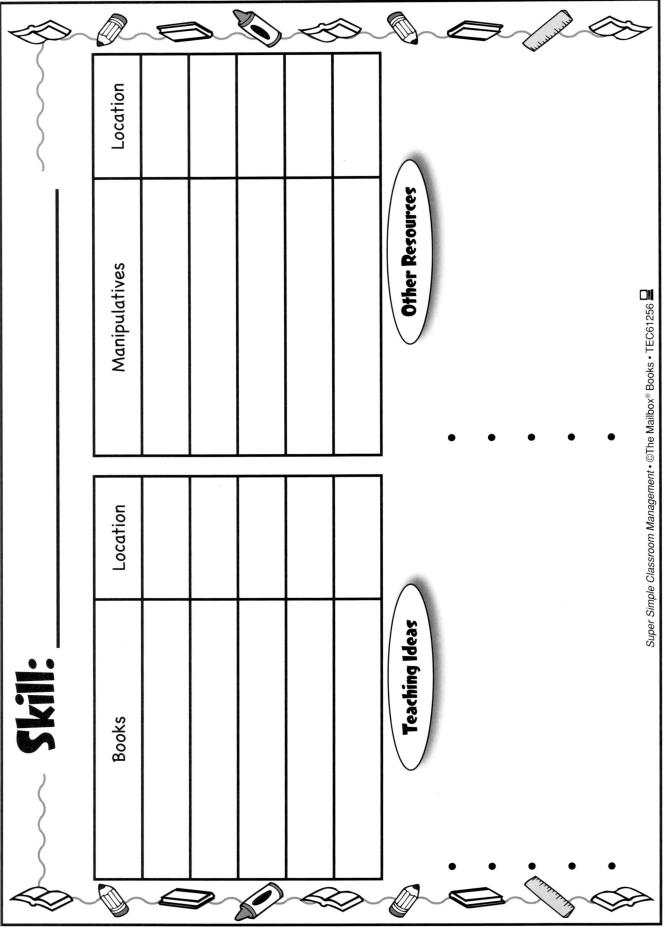

# Skill:

| Books | Location |
|-------|----------|
|       |          |
|       |          |
|       |          |
|       |          |
|       |          |

**Teaching Ideas**

| Manipulatives | Location |
|---------------|----------|
|               |          |
|               |          |
|               |          |
|               |          |
|               |          |

**Other Resources**

*Super Simple Classroom Management* • ©The Mailbox® Books • TEC61256

**Note to the teacher:** Use with "Everything You Need" on page 75.

# Student Information

Name: _____ Date of birth: _____

Address: _____

Parent/guardian: _____

Home: _____ Work: _____ Cell: _____

Email address: _____

Parent/guardian: _____

Home: _____ Work: _____ Cell: _____

Email address: _____

Emergency contact: _____
                        name                              phone

Transportation to and from school:

___walks     ___rides bus (#_____ ) other: _____

Allergies: _____

Other medical information: _____

_____

Additional information:

*Super Simple Classroom Management* • ©The Mailbox® Books • TEC61256

# Parent Conferences

## Sail Through Conferences

Use the acronym shown to remind you of key points to discuss during a parent conference. Write notes on a copy of page 80 to assist you during the conference. Then complete the remaining sections of the form during or after the conference.

**S** = Share three positive observations.

**A** = Acknowledge areas of student's strengths.

**I** = Inform the family of concerns.

**L** = Listen to the family's comments, questions, and concerns.

**S** = Set goals for the student.

## Wristband Reminders

Make a class supply of the watch patterns on page 81, cut them apart, and label each one with a different student's name. Then write the date and time of each child's parent conference on a watch. The day before a scheduled conference, tape each student's watch around his wrist to wear home.

## A Worthwhile Welcome

To create an atmosphere that will make conferences a positive experience for parents, try these tips.
- Display your name on the door for parents to easily locate your room.
- Set up a waiting area with chairs, textbooks, or other materials of interest for parents who arrive early.
- Display a sample of each student's best work.
- Group chairs to form a meeting area where you and the parents can sit together comfortably and share their child's work.

## "Tea-rific" Parents

Guide each child to fold a 6" x 12" piece of paper in half horizontally and make three cuts in the top half to create four equal flaps. On each flap, have the student draw a picture that shows why her parent is terrific and, under each flap, write a sentence about the picture. Lead each student to wrap the paper around a foam drinking cup, tape the ends together, and put a tea bag inside the cup. Give each cup to that child's parent on conference day.

See page 81 for a conference request form and page 82 for a thank-you letter to send home after a conference.

# Conference Planning Sheet

Student's name _____

Conference date and time _____

_____

## People Attending

| Name | Relationship to Student |
|---|---|
| 1. | |
| 2. | |
| 3. | |
| 4. | |

**S**hare three positive observations.

**A**reas of strength:

**I**nform family of your concerns:

**L**isten to family:

**S**et goals for the student:

*Super Simple Classroom Management* • ©The Mailbox® Books • TEC61256

80    **Note to the teacher:** Use with "Sail Through Conferences" on page 79.

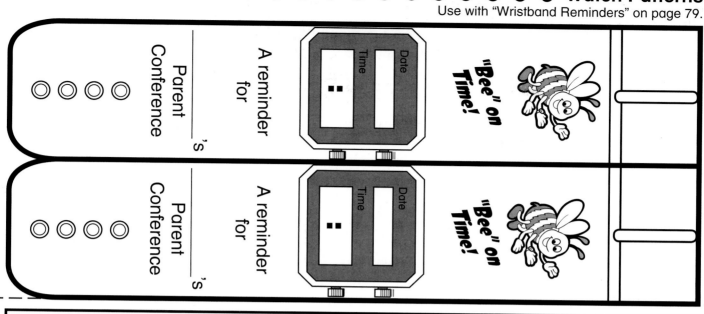

A reminder for Parent Conference ___'s

"Bee" on Time!

Date    Time

## CONFERENCE REQUEST

Student _____

Conference requested by _____

Conference date and time _____

Reason for the conference: _____

_____

_____

_____    _____
teacher's signature                      date

☐ I am able to schedule a conference at this time.

☐ I am not able to schedule a conference at this time.
   Please call to reschedule. My number is _____.

Student name _____

_____    _____
parent/guardian signature                date

*Super Simple Classroom Management* • ©The Mailbox® Books • TEC61256

**Note to the teacher:** Send a colorful copy of this form home to schedule conferences with parents or guardians. Have the student return the bottom portion of the form to school.

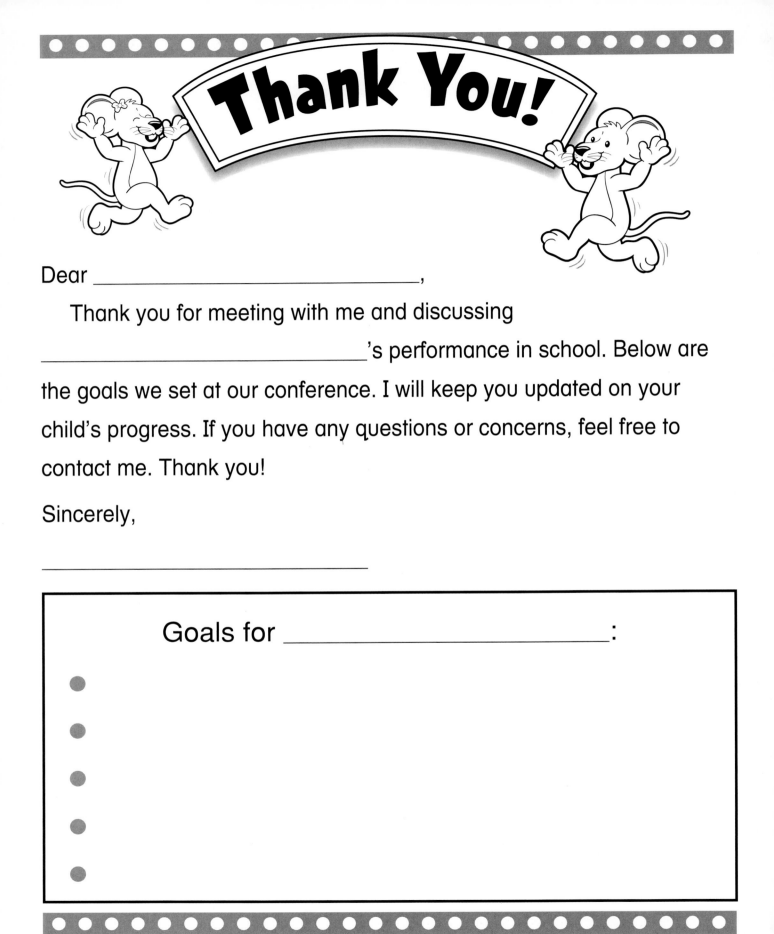

# Thank You!

Dear _____,

    Thank you for meeting with me and discussing _____'s performance in school. Below are the goals we set at our conference. I will keep you updated on your child's progress. If you have any questions or concerns, feel free to contact me. Thank you!

Sincerely,

_____

Goals for _____:

- 
- 
- 
- 
- 

**Note to the teacher:** Personalize a color copy of this page for each student to take home to his family.

# Partnering With Parents

### A Tote for Notes

Glue a small manila envelope on the inside cover of each student's assignment book or take-home folder. Anytime a student brings a note to school or takes a note home, he stores it inside the envelope.

### Share Your Day

Include a reminder with each child's daily homework by completing the sentence "Ask me about _____." Encourage each student to talk with her parents about the event featured in the sentence.

### Sticking With It

Brightly colored sticky notes are a great way to draw attention to a specific paper or assignment. Write on a sticky note the date and a brief message to the parent. Leave space on the note for the parent to write a comment and sign. When the signed note is returned, place it in your files as a record of your correspondence.

### Managing Correspondences

Make a copy of the parent communication log on page 84 for each student and keep the pages in a binder. Add plastic sheet protector pockets between each log. When you receive a parent message, store the note or a copy of the email inside the pocket and record your response on the log.

See page 85 for two helpful forms.

# Parent Communication Log

## Communication Code
E = email    P = phone
C = conference    N = note or letter

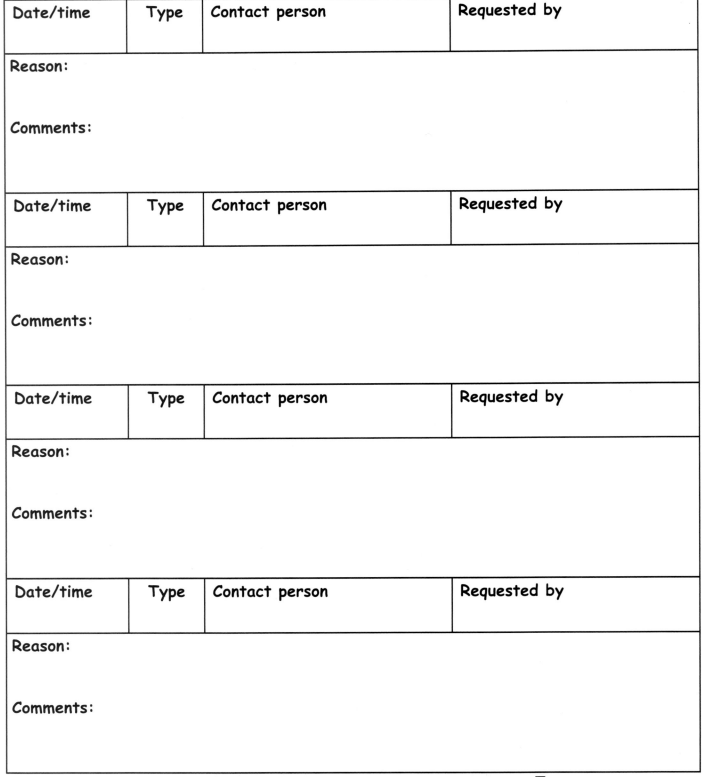

| Date/time | Type | Contact person | Requested by |
|-----------|------|----------------|--------------|

Reason:

Comments:

| Date/time | Type | Contact person | Requested by |
|-----------|------|----------------|--------------|

Reason:

Comments:

| Date/time | Type | Contact person | Requested by |
|-----------|------|----------------|--------------|

Reason:

Comments:

| Date/time | Type | Contact person | Requested by |
|-----------|------|----------------|--------------|

Reason:

Comments:

*Super Simple Classroom Management* • ©The Mailbox® Books • TEC61256

84    **Note to the teacher:** Use with "Managing Correspondences" on page 83.

## A Friendly Reminder

Please help _____

remember _____

_____

_____

_____

Thank you!

_____
teacher

_____
date

Super Simple Classroom Management • ©The Mailbox® Books • TEC61256

# Please Help

Dear Family,

_____ needs extra help with _____

_____

Following are some ways you can help your child at home:

_____

_____

_____

Thank you for your cooperation!

Sincerely,

_____          _____
teacher's signature                    date

Super Simple Classroom Management • ©The Mailbox® Books • TEC61256

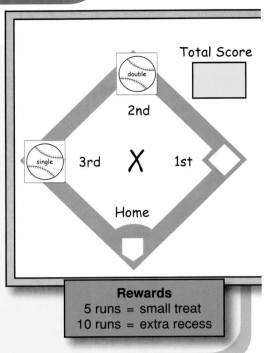

Total Score

2nd

3rd  X  1st

Home

**Rewards**
5 runs = small treat
10 runs = extra recess

## A Team Motivator

Copy page 88 on card stock, cut out the baseball cards, and place them in a ball cap. Also draw on the board a baseball diamond, like the one shown, and post a list of rewards. When the class behaves in a positive way, a student selects a card from the cap and tapes it on the appropriate base. (The student advances other cards on the diamond before he places his card on the board.) When a card reaches home plate, add one run to the class's score and return the card to the cap. If a negative class behavior occurs, draw an X (strike) on the diamond. After three strikes, the class's score is erased and the game starts over.

## Chain of Kindness

Keep a supply of colored paper strips in an accessible area, designating a different color for each month. Write the current month on a strip and make it the starter link by stapling the two ends together. Anytime your class receives a compliment from a staff member, parent volunteer, or other adult, reward students with a paper strip. Have a student write the date on a strip and add the link to the chain. Keep track of your class's monthly progress by hanging the chains side by side.

## High Five Behavior

Give each student a die-cut hand with positive character traits written on each finger and the thumb. Have the child write his name on the palm and tape the hand to his desk. When he demonstrates one of the five positive behaviors, put a small star sticker by the matching trait. When all five fingers have a sticker, display the hand on a board titled "Look Who Deserves a High Five."

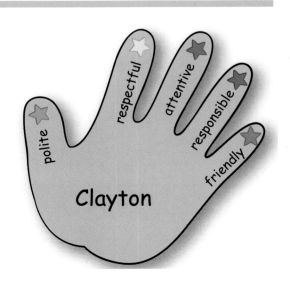

## Cooperative Groups

To remind students how to work in cooperative groups, display the acronym "SCORE." Then give each group a paper strip like the one shown. Before starting an activity, choose one of the acronym's letters and its meaning as a goal. At the end of the activity, direct only those groups that demonstrated the goal to color in the corresponding letter on their strips. Remind students who did not color the letter that they will have another opportunity once all the other letters have been called. Repeat the procedure for each group activity. When a group has colored all five letters, reward each child in the group with a small prize and give him a new strip.

**S** = Share ideas and materials.
**C** = Consider the feelings of others.
**O** = Obey the rules.
**R** = Respect property.
**E** = Encourage others in the group.

## The "Bee-Good" Game

Choose a small privilege or reward for the class and draw on the board a line for each letter in its name. Each day the class exhibits good behavior during recess, have a student guess a missing letter. If the guess is correct, write the letter on the appropriate line or lines. If the guess is incorrect or the class behaves poorly at recess, draw one body part of a bee below the lines. The class earns the privilege or reward when its name is spelled out but loses it if the bee is completed first.

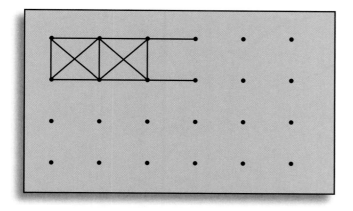

## The Compliments Connection

Create a dot grid, like the one shown, and laminate it. Each time the class is caught being good, select a student to connect two dots on the grid. If the connected lines make a square, direct the child to mark an X inside it. Reward the class when there are ten squares connected horizontally, vertically, or diagonally.

## Mystery Student Sticks

Label one plastic cup "boys" and another "girls." Write each student's name on a different craft stick and place each stick in the corresponding cup. Before the class lines up to enter the hallway, select one stick from each cup, keeping the names secret. If the selected students demonstrate good hallway behavior, give them a small reward when they return to the room.

See page 89 for a good news poster. Write a description of a student's accomplishment and add his photo. Also see page 91 for a behavior log, page 92 for an incentive chart, and page 93 for a weekly progress report.

# Baseball Cards ● ● ● ● ● ● ● ● ● ● ● ● ● ● ● ● ● ● ●

Use with "A Team Motivator" on page 86.

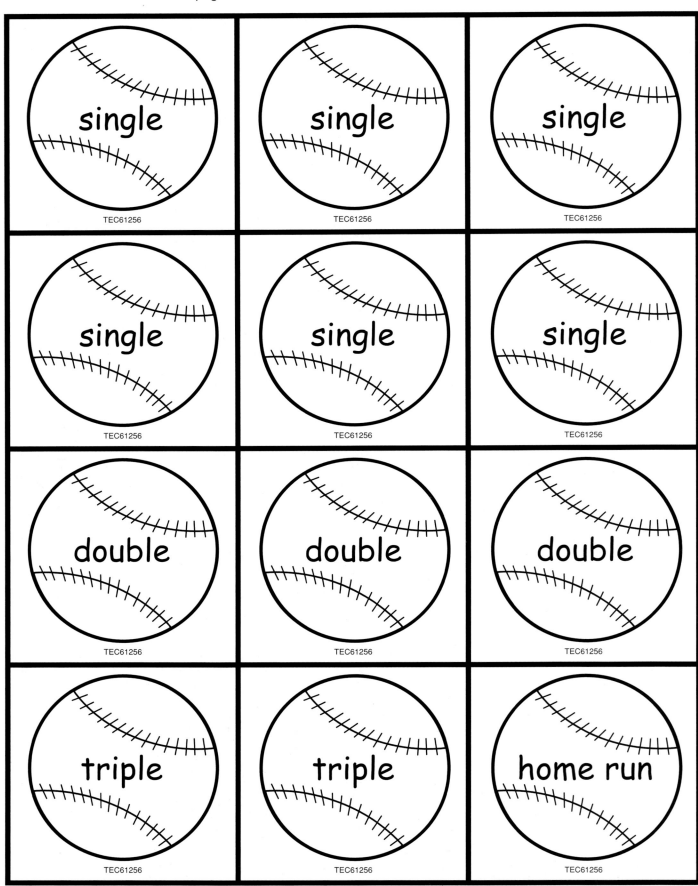

*Super Simple Classroom Management* • ©The Mailbox® Books • TEC61256

# Did you hear the GREAT news?

TIGERS

**Outstanding Student of the Week**

All-star's name _____

# My Daily Scorecard

HR = Home Run     O = Warning     X = Strike

| | Work Habits | Behavior | Organization | |
|---|---|---|---|---|
| **Monday** | | | | |
| **Tuesday** | | | | |
| **Wednesday** | | | | |
| **Thursday** | | | | |
| **Friday** | | | | |

Comments: _____

Dear Parent: Please write your initials in the box after reviewing your child's daily performance report.

*Super Simple Classroom Management* • ©The Mailbox® Books • TEC61256

---

All-star's name _____

# My Daily Scorecard

HR = Home Run     O = Warning     X = Strike

| | Work Habits | Behavior | Organization | |
|---|---|---|---|---|
| **Monday** | | | | |
| **Tuesday** | | | | |
| **Wednesday** | | | | |
| **Thursday** | | | | |
| **Friday** | | | | |

Comments: _____

Dear Parent: Please write your initials in the box after reviewing your child's daily performance report.

*Super Simple Classroom Management* • ©The Mailbox® Books • TEC61256

**Note to the teacher:** Give each student a copy of the scorecard at the beginning of the week. Each day, record students' scores. Have your students take their scorecards home each night for their parents to initial. Keep the returned scorecards for your records.

# On My Way to 20!

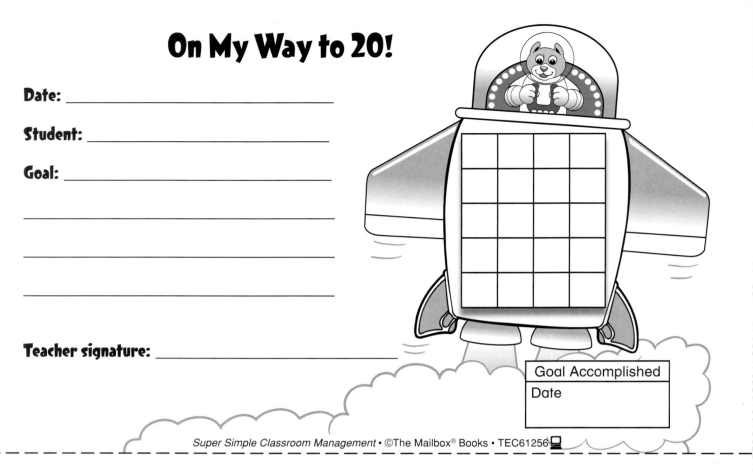

**Date:** _____

**Student:** _____

**Goal:** _____

_____

_____

_____

**Teacher signature:** _____

Goal Accomplished

Date

# On My Way to 20!

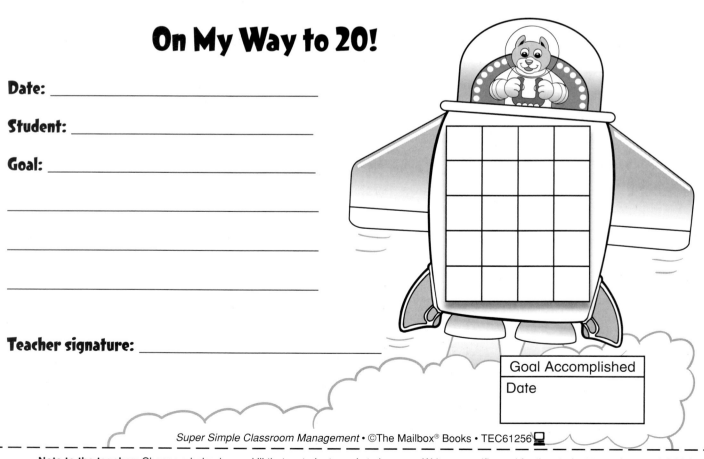

**Date:** _____

**Student:** _____

**Goal:** _____

_____

_____

_____

**Teacher signature:** _____

Goal Accomplished

Date

**Note to the teacher:** Choose a behavior or skill that a student needs to improve. Write a specific goal for the student to work toward. Initial one square for each day the goal is met. After the student receives 20 teacher initials, write the date of the accomplished goal, make a copy of the form for your records, and then send the form home.

# Weekly Progress Report

Student name _____

Week of _____

| Student Goals | Rating | Comment |
|---|---|---|
| 1. | 5  4  3  2  1 | |
| 2. | 5  4  3  2  1 | |
| 3. | 5  4  3  2  1 | |
| 4. | 5  4  3  2  1 | |
| 5. | 5  4  3  2  1 | |

5 = Excellent     4 = Very good     3 = Good     2 = Average     1 = Needs improvement

Sign and return the report to school. Please contact me if you have any questions or concerns.

_____   _____       _____   _____
teacher's signature              date                  parent's signature              date

*Super Simple Classroom Management* • ©The Mailbox® Books • TEC61256 💻

- - - - - - - - - - - - - - - - - - - - - - - - - - - - - - - - - - - - - - - - - - - - - - - - -

# Weekly Progress Report

Student name _____

Week of _____

| Student Goals | Rating | Comment |
|---|---|---|
| 1. | 5  4  3  2  1 | |
| 2. | 5  4  3  2  1 | |
| 3. | 5  4  3  2  1 | |
| 4. | 5  4  3  2  1 | |
| 5. | 5  4  3  2  1 | |

5 = Excellent     4 = Very good     3 = Good     2 = Average     1 = Needs improvement

Sign and return the report to school. Please contact me if you have any questions or concerns.

_____   _____       _____   _____
teacher's signature              date                  parent's signature              date

*Super Simple Classroom Management* • ©The Mailbox® Books • TEC61256 💻

**Note to the teacher:** Each week, make a class supply of this form. Complete a form for each student and send it home at the end of the week.

### Substitute on Duty

Color a copy of the door hanger pattern on page 95; then laminate it and cut it out. Display the hanger on the outside knob of your classroom door to let colleagues and visitors know a substitute is in your room.

### Plans in a Pinch

Label one of five different-colored folders for each day of the week. Include in each folder the day's schedule and specific details about daily routines. Also put in a supply of extra worksheets and assignments that are appropriate for that day of the week. Store the folders in an easy-to-find place in case a substitute teacher needs to be called in at the last minute.

### A Positive Report

Put a class list inside your substitute teacher folder. Have the substitute draw stars next to the name of each student that was helpful and cooperative. When you return to school, acknowledge those students with a small reward, privilege, or word of praise.

### Surprise Box

In advance, wrap the lid of a shirt gift box with wrapping paper. Program a copy of the letter on page 95 with the substitute's name and sign the letter. Put the letter and a storybook that the class has not heard inside the box. Leave a note with your substitute plans that directs the substitute to read the letter and the book to the class.

See page 96 for a checklist to help you plan for a substitute teacher.

Super Substitute on Duty

TEC61256

Dear Boys and Girls,

　　I will not be in school today. _____ is here to help you while I'm away. Please be on your best behavior and be helpful. I planned to read a special book to you today. Since I am not able to read it to you, I'm glad _____ can. Enjoy the story! I'll see you very soon.

　　　　Sincerely,

TEC61256

*Super Simple Classroom Management* • ©The Mailbox® Books • TEC61256

**Note to the teacher:** Use with "Surprise Box" on page 94.

95

# Substitute Teacher Checklist

## Last Updated

| | |
|---|---|
| ☐ September _____ | ☐ February _____ |
| ☐ October _____ | ☐ March _____ |
| ☐ November _____ | ☐ April _____ |
| ☐ December _____ | ☐ May _____ |
| ☐ January _____ | ☐ June _____ |

## The following are included in this folder:

☐ Class list

☐ Seating chart

☐ Student medical needs

☐ Student dismissal list

☐ IEP/modified students

☐ Student pullouts
(speech, reading, math)

☐ Class schedule

☐ Classroom procedures

☐ Behavior/discipline plan

☐ "Where to Find It"

☐ Duty schedules

☐ School map

☐ Faculty list

☐ School handbook

☐ Safety plans
(fire, emergency, severe weather)

☐ Other _____

☐ Other _____

**Note to the teacher:** Make a copy of this checklist and keep it inside your substitute teacher folder. At the beginning of each month, review the contents of the folder and update the folder with current information.

### Saving Time

Set a timer with the amount of time you think is suitable for your class to transition between activities. At the beginning of a transition, start the timer; then stop it when all your students are settled and ready. If the timer has any time remaining on it, record the amount on the board. Keep a running record of the time saved throughout the week. Then, at the end of the week give students a fun activity to do with the time they saved.

## Respectful Listeners

Get students' attention with the following chant. Your class will know they are expected to listen when the chant is finished.

> **Teacher:** R-E-S-P
> **Students:** E-C-T.
> **All:** Show me what it means to be—respectful!

## Fun Time Fillers

Cut apart the task cards on pages 99–106 and store them in a basket. Use the cards any time there are five or ten minutes of free time. Simply select a card, read the directions aloud, and allow time for students to complete the task.

## First Dibs

Each time the class switches from one activity to another, place a small stuffed animal on the desk of the student who is ready first and give the child a sticker.

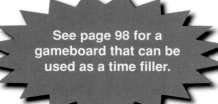

See page 98 for a gameboard that can be used as a time filler.

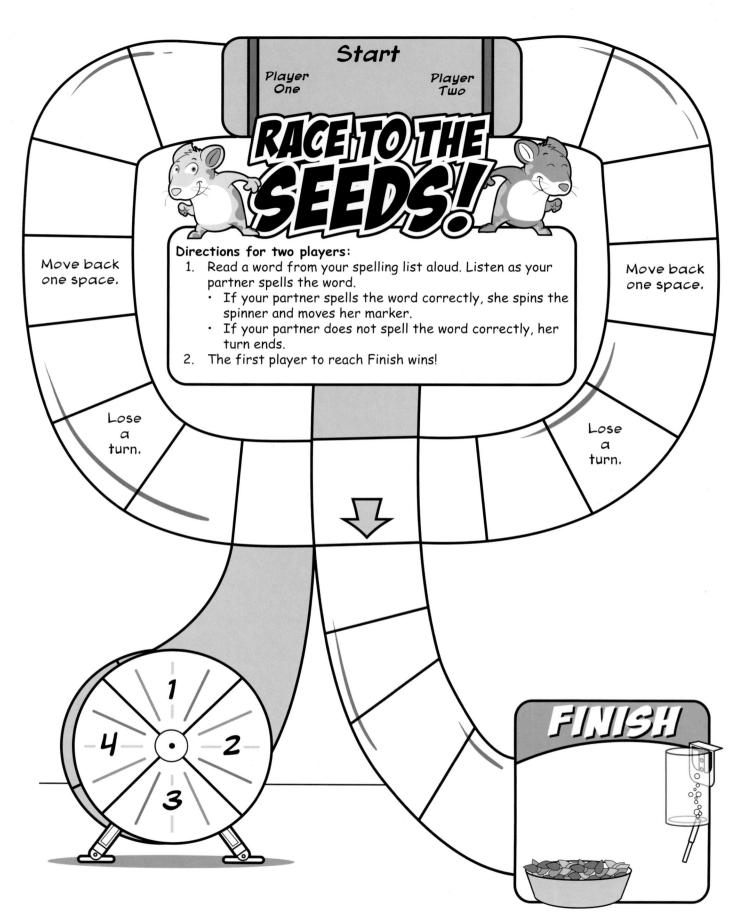

## Start

Player One

Player Two

# RACE TO THE SEEDS!

**Directions for two players:**
1. Read a word from your spelling list aloud. Listen as your partner spells the word.
   - If your partner spells the word correctly, she spins the spinner and moves her marker.
   - If your partner does not spell the word correctly, her turn ends.
2. The first player to reach Finish wins!

Move back one space.

Move back one space.

Lose a turn.

Lose a turn.

**FINISH**

*Super Simple Classroom Management* • ©The Mailbox® Books • TEC61256

**Note to the teacher:** Make student copies of the gameboard and keep them in an accessible place. Have students use a pencil and paper clip to spin. As an added challenge, students may also use this gameboard to review math facts or vocabulary words.

# Number Toss

Choose two students to each roll a pair of dice.
Write on the board the number that each student rolls.
Then write an operation.
Have each student write a word problem using the two numbers and the operation.
Direct each student to exchange his paper with a partner.

10   8

multiply

Farmer Ted has 8 chickens. Each chicken lays 10 eggs. How many eggs do the chickens lay altogether?

# What If?

Ask students to imagine one of the following situations. Have each student turn to a partner and share what she would do in the situation.

1. Your television does not work.
2. You've won a million dollars.
3. Your favorite holiday will no longer be celebrated.
4. You will be principal for a day.
5. You've been invited to meet the president.

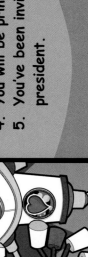

# Name Game

Write the first and last name of a student on the board.
Have students use the letters to write as many words as they can.

Jonathan Smith

this

hat    most

# A Great Invention

Guide students to brainstorm household chores.
Direct each student to invent a machine that could do one chore.
Have the child draw a picture of the machine and write a few sentences explaining how it works.

Master Bed-Maker 3000
My machine uses six different robotic arms to tuck in the sheets, fluff the pillows, and fold blankets all at the same time. It is fast and can make a bed in less than a minute.
Michael

**Note to the teacher:** Use with "Fun Time Fillers" on page 97.

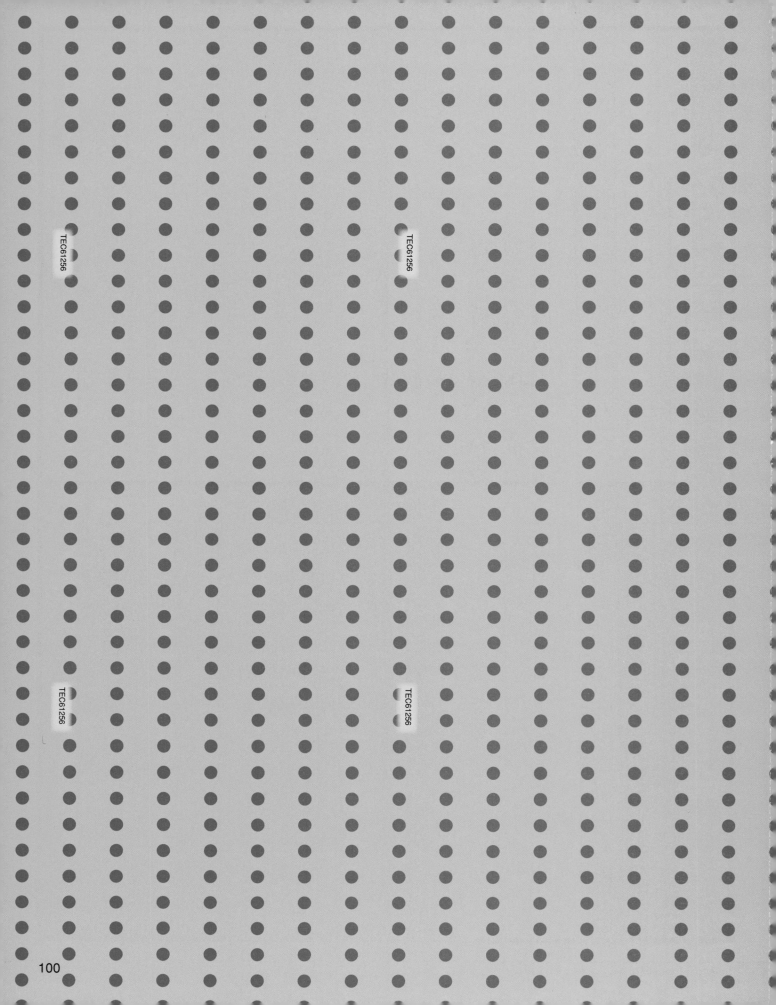

# Calendar Curiosity

Have students look at the classroom calendar.
Ask them the following questions.

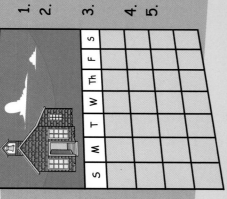

1. How many days are in this month?
2. On what days does this month begin and end?
3. On what day will next month begin?
4. On what day did last month end?
5. How do the numbers of Mondays and Fridays compare?

# Winding Words

Challenge students to name as many animals as they can. Have one student start by stating an animal's name. Then have the next student name an animal using the last letter of the previous animal's name. Continue until no more animals can be named. Challenge students in the same way with other topics.

Skunk.

Kangaroo.

Tiger.

Rhinoceros.

Dog.

Goat.

# What's in There?

Name a room in a house or a school.
Have student pairs brainstorm lists of items that could be found in that room.
Give students a time limit for writing their lists.

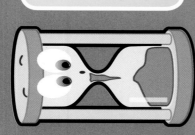

### Rooms

- kitchen
- bedroom
- living room
- bathroom
- classroom
- principal's office
- gym
- cafeteria

# It's Symmetrical

Have students take turns pointing to objects in the classroom that are symmetrical.
Then have the student tell how many lines of symmetry the object has.

---

*Super Simple Classroom Management* • ©The Mailbox® Books • TEC61256

**Note to the teacher:** Use with "Fun Time Fillers" on page 97.

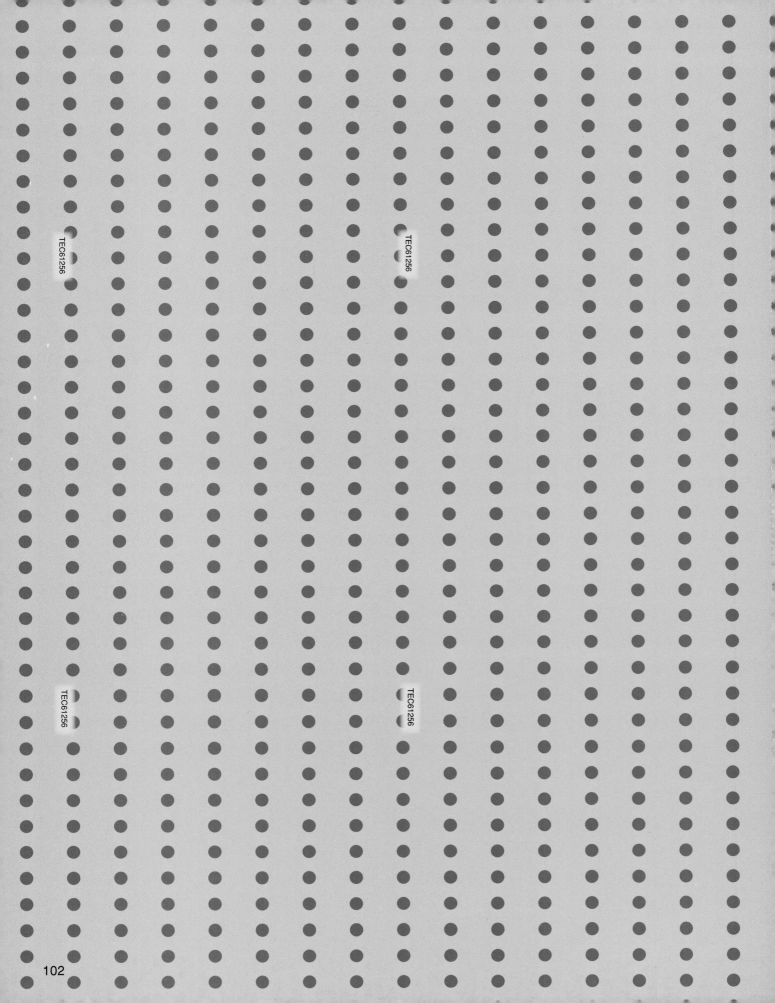

## 4...3...2...1

Have each student work with a partner and list things that are associated with the numbers 4, 3, 2, and 1.

| 4 | 3 | 2 | 1 |
|---|---|---|---|
| legs on a chair | wheels on a tricycle | wings on a bird | nose on my face |

## New School Mascot

Direct each student to draw a new mascot for the school. Have the child explain the reason for his choice.

Walnut Street Elementary Owls
An owl has very good eyesight.
Our owl mascot would keep an eye on us.

## Kindness Day

Direct students to pretend it is Kindness Day. Have groups of students list ten ways people can be kind to each other.

Kindness Day

1. Hold the door for someone.
2. Tell someone they look nice.
3. Share a snack with your friend.

## Make Change

Announce a monetary amount up to $1.00. Have students name the different coin combinations that can make up that amount. Write the combinations on the board.

87¢

3 quarters, 1 dime, 2 pennies
3 quarters, 2 nickels, 2 pennies
3 quarters, 12 pennies

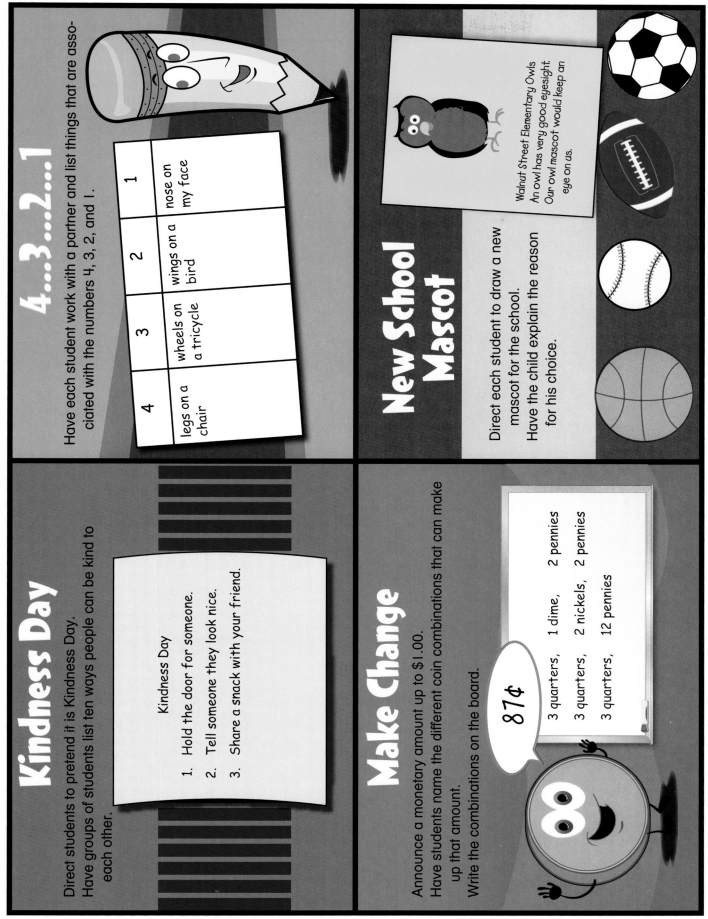

*Super Simple Classroom Management* • ©The Mailbox® Books • TEC61256

**Note to the teacher:** Use with "Fun Time Fillers" on page 97.

103

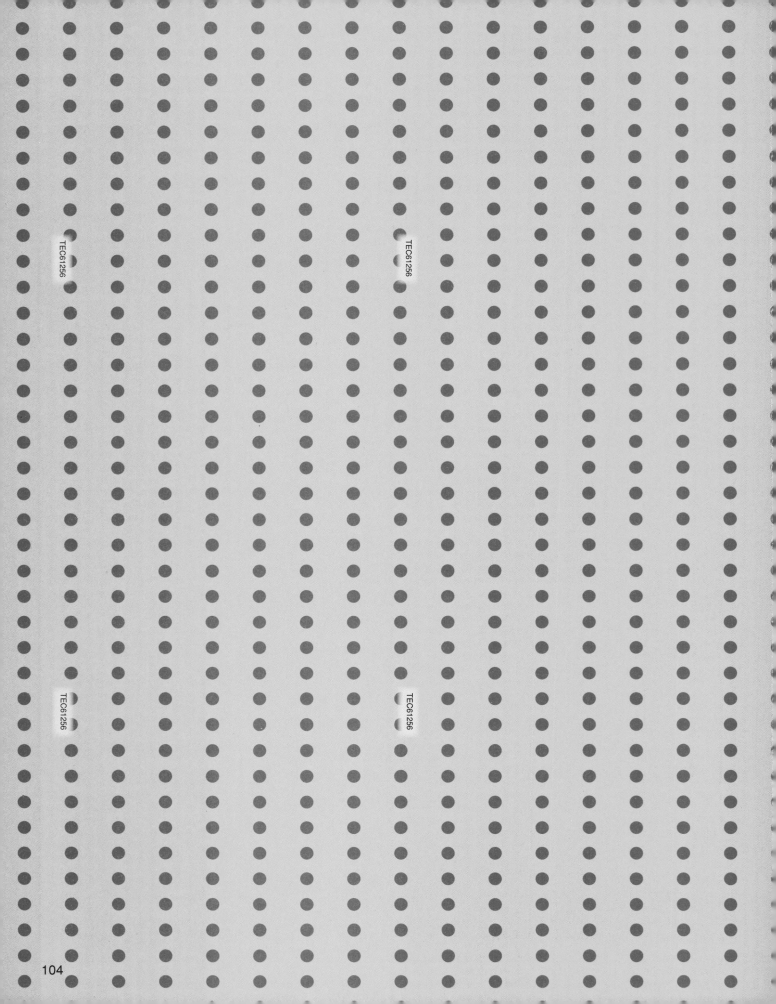

# What's Different?

Write a sentence on the board.

Have students read the sentence and then turn around so they can't see the board.

Change a letter in one of the words in the sentence.

Direct students to turn back around and look for the letter that was changed.

Have a student point to the letter that was changed.

The people waited in line to buy tickets.

# The 5 Ws

Write the title of a school event or classroom happening on the board.

Direct each student to turn to a partner and share what she recalls about the event.

Have each child write an answer to each of these five questions.

Field Trip to the Zoo

Who?
What?
When?
Where?
Why?

# Guess My Number

Think of a number between 100 and 200 and write it on a piece of paper.

Go around the room and ask each student to guess your number.

Respond to each incorrect guess with "Too high" or "Too low."

Stop the game when a student guesses the correct number.

143?

# Quick Draw

Announce a scene, such as a city, beach, or restaurant. Set a time limit.

Direct each student to draw as many items that belong in that scene as he can.

When time is up, allow students to share their pictures with a partner.

*Super Simple Classroom Management* • ©The Mailbox® Books • TEC61256

**Note to the teacher:** Use with "Fun Time Fillers" on page 97.

105

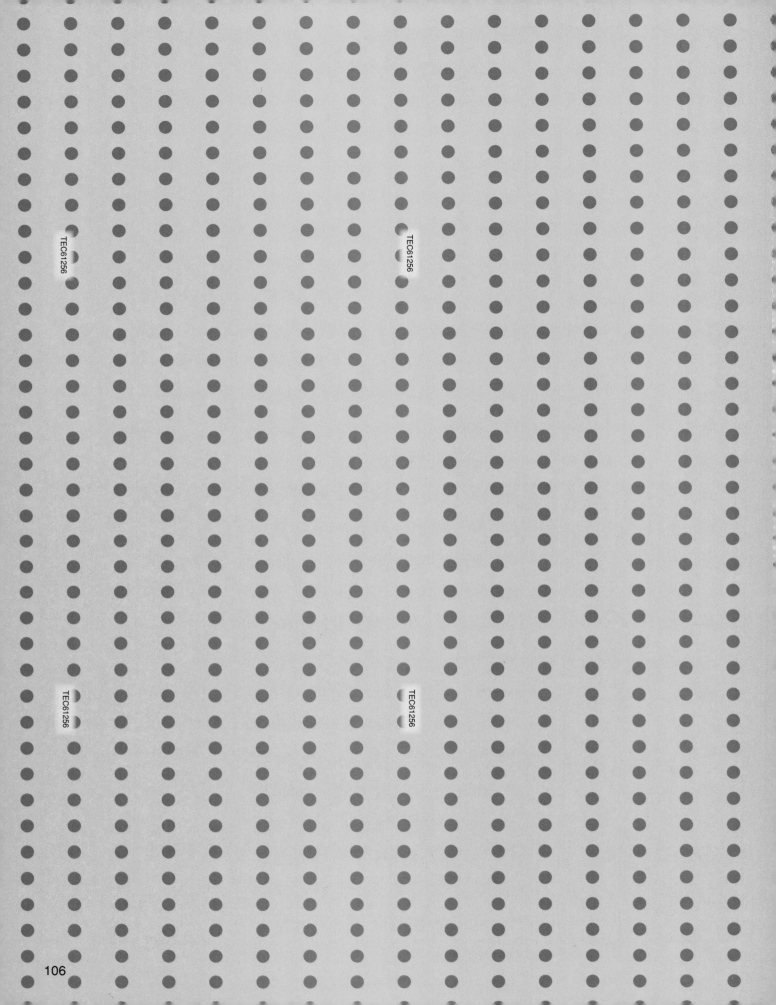

# Welcoming New Students

## Welcoming Committee

In advance, make a grid like the one shown. Assign two children to complete one of the tasks with a student new to the class. After they complete the task, have the new student mark an X on the square. Then assign two more children to complete another task in the same manner. Continue until all the tasks on the grid are completed.

| Show and Tell Our New Classmate... | | |
|---|---|---|
| How to find the nurse's office | Who the specials teachers are and what each one teaches | Where our class sits for lunch |
| What we play at recess | How to find the school library | How to use the classroom library |
| Where the school's lost and found is | What games are on the classroom computer | Where bus riders and car riders go at the end of the day |

## Getting to Know Everyone

Each day assign a different student to be a new student's buddy. Cut out a copy of the buttons from page 108 and personalize them for the students to wear. Have the buddy assist the new student as he learns the class's routine and his way around the school.

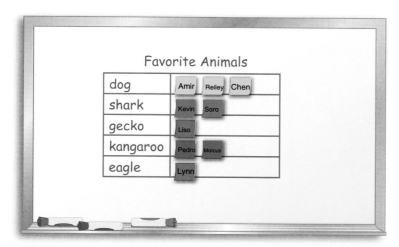

Favorite Animals

| dog | Amir | Reiley | Chen |
| shark | Kevin | Sara | |
| gecko | Lisa | | |
| kangaroo | Pedro | Marcus | |
| eagle | Lynn | | |

## Something in Common

During a new student's first week of school, make a graph on the board that shows at least five of her favorite animals, foods, games, books, etc. Then invite each child to write her name on a sticky note and place it on the graph next to her choice.

## Classroom Manual

Have your class make a book that can be shared with new students as they arrive. Direct each child to illustrate and write a page that tells one thing a new student might want to know about your classroom or school. Bind the pages into a book and present it to your new student.

See page 108 for a card to welcome a new student to your class.

# New Buddy Buttons

Use with "Getting to Know Everyone" on page 107.

(new student's buddy)

(new student)

**Note to the teacher:** Copy the card on card stock. Write a welcome message on the back and have each student sign the card.

# At the End of the Year

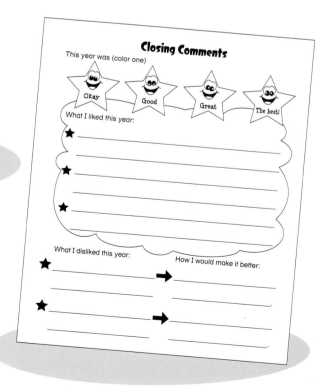

### Editor's Pick

## Fresh and Clean

At the end of the school year, use nontoxic cleaning supplies to spruce up your class-room. Sprinkle baking soda on pencil, ink, crayon, or marker stains and then rub them away gently. Sponge white vinegar on stickers or tape marks and wait about 15 minutes before wiping away the mess.

## Closing Comments

Invite each student to reflect on the school year and consider what he liked and disliked about things such as the classroom layout, rules, routines, and decorations; then have each child anonymously complete a copy of page 111. Consider students' responses when planning for next year.

## Memorable Events

Have each student glue a photo taken during the school year to a copy of page 112. Direct each child to write a description of the activity related to the photo and then staple the completed pages together to make a class book. No photos available? No problem! Have each child draw pictures of favorite school year memories instead.

## Reorganization

To get your reproducibles in order for next year, label several file folders with the skills or standards you teach. On the back of each reproducible master, write the corresponding label. When you're ready to file the paper, you'll know just where it goes!

# Closing Comments

This year was (color one)

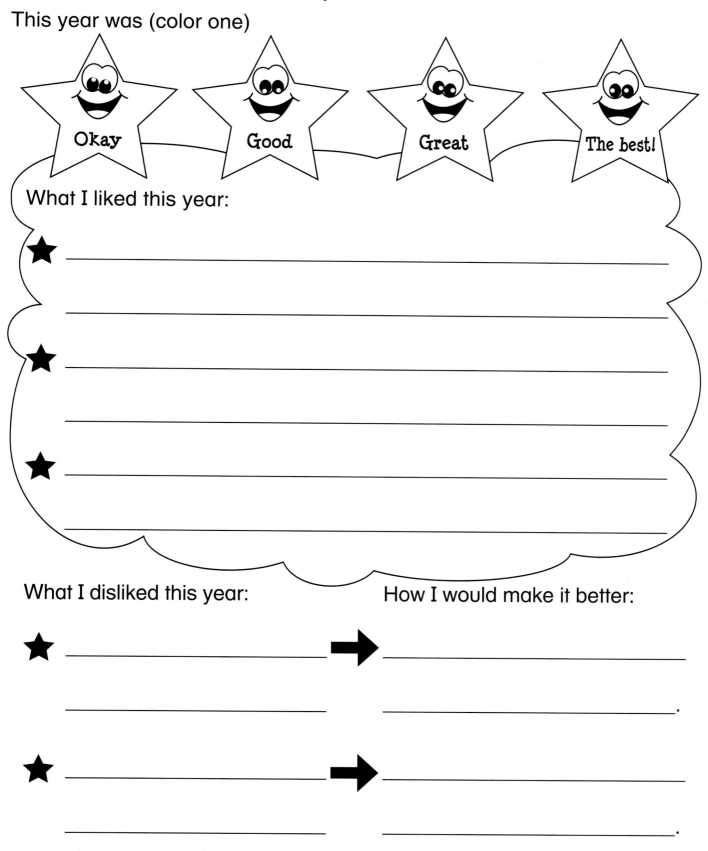

Okay     Good     Great     The best!

What I liked this year:

★ _____

_____

★ _____

_____

★ _____

_____

What I disliked this year:     How I would make it better:

★ _____ ➡ _____

_____ _____ .

★ _____ ➡ _____

_____ _____ .

**I remember...**

by _____

**Note to the teacher:** Use with "Memorable Events" on page 110.